BATHROOM STYLES

ALLISON MURRAY MORRIS

CONSULTANT: ELLEN FRANKEL

PUBLICATIONS INTERNATIONAL, LTD.

ISBN: 0-7853-1273-0

ALLISON MURRAY MORRIS

CONSULTANT: ELLEN FRANKEL

Allison Murray Morris is former editor of *Woman's Day Kitchens & Baths, Woman's Day Home Decorating Ideas,* and *American HomeStyle Kitchen & Bath Planner.* She has covered the kitchen and bath industry extensively for both consumer and trade publications concentrating on home improvements and remodeling.

Ellen Frankel is former editor-in-chief of *1,001 Home Ideas* and former home-design editor of *McCall's.* She serves as consulting editor of home-furnishing features for several consumer publications. She is president of ECPM, Inc., editorial and marketing consultants specializing in the home-design field.

CONTENTS

INTRODUCTION

Building a new bathroom is a lot like putting together a jigsaw puzzle. It doesn't happen overnight. The design is usually a culmination of weeks, months, or sometimes even years of planning.

The best way to get started on your new bath is to look at

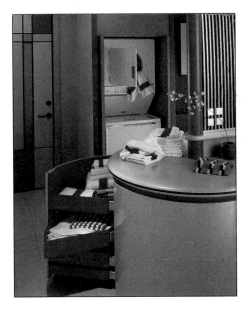

other baths. You've probably seen friends' and relatives' updated spaces that may or may not suit your taste. Finding out what you don't like is just as important as establishing what you do. That's why *Bathroom Styles* should get you off to a good start. You aren't going to like everything you see photographed in this book. And you shouldn't.

As you look through *Bathroom Styles,* which is organized into 10 different bath-design sections, jot

down some of your opinions. Don't forget to include a list

of those things you must have and those things you'd like to

have. This will give you a portfolio of ideas to take along

when you start shopping for products or begin interviewing

professionals to help you out.

And don't be confused if you "fall in love" with several

very different baths showcased in *Bathroom Styles*. If you

keep looking at products and designs, eventually you'll

narrow down what you really want and what's realistic.

If not, remember that with a little creativity

almost anything can be combined. Good luck

creating your dream bath!

GEOMETRICAL PATTERNS

Mixing and matching shapes and materials can add interest to any bathroom, as is evident in these two spaces. The modern bath showcased on this page dares to be different, from its curved vanity to the triangular pillar that works as a type of room divider. There's marble on the countertop, tile on the floor, wood cabinets, and plenty of glass. Separate pieces of cherry furniture provide drawers for toiletries, while adding a unique design element.

An interesting combination of windows and tile is an eye-catcher in the green-and-white bath. This space offers all the extras, including a sit-down makeup area, drawers for storage, and a towel warmer. The oval tub is perfect for long, relaxing soaks. The light decor adds to the room's spacious feel.

ROOMY VANITY

A variety of shapes and materials team up to create the dramatic grooming area above. Using furniture for storage allows for easy updating in years to come. Sink: Hastings. Marble: Michigan Tile and Marble Company. Cabinets: Madison Design Group.

GLASS WORKS

Natural light cascades into an oversize shower (right), lowered to keep the rest of the bathroom dry. The glass enclosure makes the narrow bath appear less confining. Designer: Kenneth Neumann, FAIA. Tile: Virginia Tile Company.

SAFEKEEPING

By extending the tub platform (right), the designer was able to create a seat for entering and exiting the tub. The cabinet hides away small bath essentials. Designer: Kenneth Neumann, FAIA. Tile: Pewabic Society. Marble: Michigan Tile and Marble Company. Cabinets: Madison Design Group.

OPEN UP WITH MIRRORS

Even if space in your bathroom is limited, you don't have to settle for a design that's tight. Make it big. Start by jotting down those things you must have versus those you'd like to include. Work on your layout, fitting in what you can. Try to create a spacious feel.

The bath on these pages is a prime example of what mirrors can do to make a room feel bigger and brighter. Of course, this space is already roomy, but the mirrored wall behind the tub makes the design seem endless. The double vanity is also backed by a mirror.

There are several other contemporary features. Sleek white cabinets and a glamorous countertop team up in the double vanity. The whirlpool, therapeutic for body and soul, is wrapped in a matching platform. Step into the steam shower for further relaxation. A neutral decor makes the bath timeless.

LUXURY TUB

Angling the whirlpool (right) lends a touch of drama and maximizes space in this layout. With two contrasting finishes, adjacent storage has the look of furniture. Tub: Kohler. Fittings: Dornbracht.

MASTER TOUCHES

Side-by-side sinks (below) make sense in a bath that is often shared. The fully enclosed steam shower is an added pleasure. Designer: Jackie Naylor, CKD, Allied ASID. Sinks: Kohler. Cabinets: SieMatic.

TOUCH OF GLASS

Round skylights and recessed lighting offer plenty of illumination in this corridor bath—not that it isn't bright to begin with. The primarily white room is covered with crisp white tile. High-gloss black countertops and matching tile borders lend a dramatic contrast.

Partitions made of tile and glass block help keep things separate, but don't break up the flow. By angling the whirlpool tub and adding a wall to separate it from the vanity, the designer built a cozy nook for long, relaxing soaks. A door closes off the toilet, but the shower is dramatic *sans* enclosure.

PRIVATE QUARTERS

At the far end of the bath, a partial wall of glass block and tile (right) separates the whirlpool and contemporary vanity. Whirlpool, sink, faucets: Eljer. Cabinets: Wood-Mode. Countertop: Wilsonart. Lighting: Halo Division of Cooper Lighting.

WATER-SAVING STEP

Things stay dry outside the doorless shower (above), thanks to its three surrounding walls and step. A glossy black stripe gives white-tile walls just the lift they need. Tile: American Olean. Shower: Eljer.

ADDING LIGHT

Glass block and round skylights open up this narrow bath (left). You hardly notice it's a windowless room! Architect: James Nagle. Designer: Candise Zake. Glass block: Pittsburgh Corning.

SPACE-SAVING SOLUTIONS

Muted colors, plenty of natural light, and well-positioned mirrors can make a space appear larger than it actually is. The three baths shown here go a bit further, though, taking full advantage of creative license.

A double vanity, a two-person shower, and an oversize whirlpool are among the amenities in the gray-and-white master bath on this page. To fit in all this and more without making the layout seem cramped, the designer created a diagonal plan consisting of various levels: Step up to the whirlpool platform, keep going, and you're at the shower.

Custom cabinetry arranged in untraditional ways makes winners of the other two baths. Angled and curved combinations allow for cabinets to be put where they couldn't have been otherwise.

EXTRA STORAGE

A curved vanity (above) fits snugly in the corner. Extra storage space has been created by raising the countertop and adding a cabinet above the toilet. Designer: Molly Ann Conroy/NKBA Design Competition 1991. Sink, countertop: DuPont Corian. Toilet: Kohler. Fittings: Grohe.

VANITY FOR TWO

Drenched in natural light, this master bath (left) has a back-to-back vanity with pentagon-shaped mirrors and a granite countertop. The varied heights and levels create an interesting contemporary look. Designer: Victoria Leist/NKBA Design Competition 1991. Cabinets: Style Line. Tile: Villeroy & Bach. Sink: Eljer. Whirlpool: Hydro Systems. Fittings: Dornbracht.

CREATIVE LAYOUT

This wraparound vanity (left) includes two sinks and storage galore, including a tall linen closet. The unique layout makes the most of limited space. *Designer: Randy Brandes/NKBA Design Competition 1991. Cabinets: Stylecraft. Sinks, countertop: DuPont Corian. Toilet, fittings: Kohler.*

A STEP ABOVE

Large windows and the clever placement of mirrors make this master-bath suite seem as if it's sitting right in the great outdoors. The natural views and ample sunlight team with white, mauve, and raspberry for a stunning result.

There's nothing missing in this bath, either. "His" and "her" vanities on opposite sides of the room offer plenty of space for pampering. One has a sit-down area for grooming. Extra cabinetry in the other keeps all the essentials organized and out of view.

Tile detailing on the floor mimics the layout of the bath. Take a look at the neoangle shower. All roads lead to the magnificent whirlpool—set in a tile-and-glass-block platform and surrounded by a palladian window and two mirrors.

PLATFORM TUB

The whirlpool (left) takes center stage. To heighten the drama, the designer backlit the two steps of tile and glass block. Builder: Coastal Development.

MAKEUP AREA

One of the bath's two vanities (top right) includes an elegant seat and open counter for "her." If the homeowner wants some privacy, she just closes the shade. Tile: American Olean. Fixtures: Kohler.

'HIS' & 'HERS'

"His" vanity, like "hers," is suspended to look as if it's floating (right). Gold accents add to the bath's elegant appeal. Designer: Betsy Godfrey.

PLAYING ALL THE ANGLES

It may not be the most spacious bathroom, but all the essentials fit right in. A whirlpool/shower combination makes the most of tight quarters. Corner shelves and a height-adjustable spray are included inside.

The toilet comfortably sits kitty-corner along the glass enclosure. Decorative storage is provided on the custom countertop that wraps above the toilet. Angling the double-door vanity, which neatly hides away shampoo, soap, and other grooming necessities, sets the room's interesting layout in motion.

The designer was able to brighten the space by vaulting the ceiling and installing a skylight. These elements, along with black-tile striping, are arresting accents in the primarily white bath. Brass accents are a nice finishing touch.

SPACE SAVER

Angling the base cabinets (left) creates much-needed storage. Black horizontal strips add a spark to the white countertop and cabinets, while highlighting the unique design. Designer: Thomas Trzcinski, CKD, CBD/NKBA Design Competition. Cabinets: Hagerstown Kitchens. Tile: Wenzel. Accessories: NuTone.

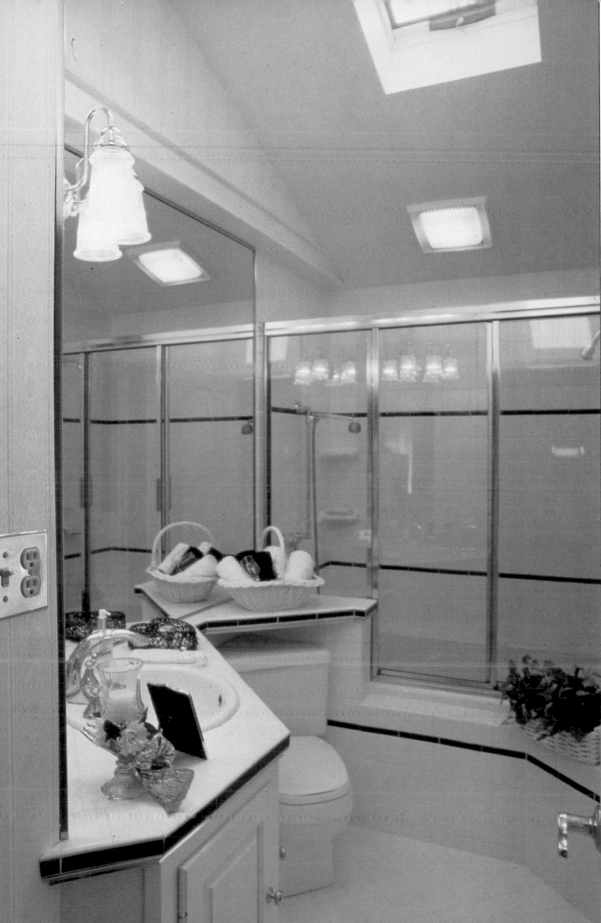

A pretty ledge above the toilet (left) has been created by extending the vanity countertop. This also allows for a larger wall mirror. *Shower: Basco. Sink, fittings: Kohler. Lighting: Juno, Velux Skylights.*

GRAND ILLUSIONS

Look at these two master baths and you'll do a double take. Both designs feature the creative use of mirror images.

One transforms a rather typical space into a marble charmer. The vanity and toilet are neatly tucked at one end, while the glass-enclosed shower takes up the other. By keeping the shower open, the bath appears less cramped. Window shutters allow for optimal control of light and privacy, while softening the room's decor.

In the other bath, an all-white double vanity is divided by a round mirror extending down from the ceiling. Center-island vanities help maximize space. A few feet away, the tub platform offers an extended area that's ideal for keeping towels dry and within reach. It also doubles as a seat.

DUAL VANITY

A center vanity (right) takes advantage of open floor space and provides for grooming areas that face each other. Rounded edges make traffic flow more comfortable. Designer: Jane Redfield Schwartz. Sinks: Kohler. Tub: Jacuzzi. Hardware: Alno.

LUXURY SHOWER

Marble creates a mirror image that opens up this small space (left). The glass-enclosed shower features a showerhead at one end and a bench and built-in storage at the other. Designer: Accent on Design.

MASTER-SUITE MASTERPIECE

Art hangs gracefully from the walls. Marble on the floor and walls creates a magnificent backdrop. Although it has a museumlike quality, this master-bath suite is warm and inviting. Rather than warning "Hands Off," it says "Welcome."

There's more to this bathroom than initially meets the eye. Two custom vanities offer extensive countertop space and storage. Wrapped around the end of one, the toilet is out of view. The marble shower's doorless design is in keeping with the flowing layout.

A skylight and recessed lighting make the master bath bright. Most striking, though, are the decorative fixtures that extend from the ceiling over the vanities.

'HIS' & 'HERS'

Two long runs of cabinetry (left) create "his" and "her" vanities. Hanging light fixtures and pictures on the walls add personal touches. Cabinets: Wood-Mode. Sinks, countertop: DuPont Corian. Fittings: American Standard. Recessed lighting: NuTone.

PRIVATE QUARTERS

Privacy is guaranteed in this cozy nook (right). Towels are neatly folded in the back of one custom vanity. To the right, stained-glass art makes a magnificent statement. Designer: Thomas Doty/NKBA Design Competition 1992. Toilet: Kohler.

EVERYDAY CROWD PLEASER

Bright and refreshing, this bath more than meets the needs of a family. There's plenty of space at the vanity, plus an oversize shower and a separate compartment for the toilet.

What makes this bath even more wonderful is safety features ideal for users of all ages. A slip-resistant tile floor, adjustable showerhead, and antiscald device make for a safe and comfortable shower. The tub is set in a platform that simplifies getting in and out. Even the windows have been carefully selected. They open with the twist of a handle—from the top rather than the bottom.

Add all this to a creamy decor with subtly colorful accents and the result is a wide-open bath that can be shared—or appreciated in private.

SAFEKEEPING

From the height-adjustable showerhead to the nonslip tile floor, this spacious shower (above) plays it safe. Shower enclosure: Glass Products International. Showerhead: American Standard. Tile: Florida Tile.

SMART COLORS

An inset resilient vinyl pattern on the floor (right) adds a playful bit of color to this family bath. The room's neutral color scheme makes it timeless. Designers: John A. Buscarello, ASID, and George Magyar, CBD. Floor: Armstrong. Tub: American Standard. Tub surround: Wilsonart.

LIKE FURNITURE

Cabinet fronts used on the tub surround (right) match the vanity, giving the tub a more built-in appeal. Cabinets: Bertch Cabinetry.

OUT IN THE OPEN

Add elegant products to a flowing plan, and you've got a luxurious retreat to enjoy on a daily basis. Two mirrored walls intersect behind the tub area, giving the illusion of an even grander view. A dramatic platform leads the way to the whirlpool set four steps above. The glass shower enclosure neatly angles over the platform, creating a small shelf for shampoo and soap.

On the opposite side of the tub, the platform stretches out to house the sink. The L-shaped vanity has a sit-down area for make-up application and other grooming tasks.

SPACIOUS PLAN

A magnificent tub platform (right) ties together several elements of this bath. The shower uses part of the platform as an inner shelf for shampoo and other bath amenities. On the opposite side, the vanity takes advantage of its sturdy base. Designer: Grayson Ltd. Fixtures: Kohler.

HOOKED ON STYLE

Not a detail is overlooked in this trio of bathing beauties. Their designs are unique and packed with decorative accents.

Taking advantage of a spectacular view, the first bath is bright and airy. The wall of windows brings the outdoors in. An oversize mirror above the crisp white vanity makes the room and the view seem even larger. The marble floor and gold accents are nice finishing touches.

A round tub sits gracefully under the dramatic vaulted ceiling and window of the second bath. Its one-of-a-kind decor includes an extensive black-and-white vanity for plenty of pampering.

Zigzag tilework on the floor creates a walkway through the third bath. The neoangle shower and vanity are customized to match. Extending from the vanity, a pretty built-in bench provides a place to sit. Royal colors in fabrics and wallcovering dress up the room.

OPEN VIEW

The bath above becomes a sunroom with its wall of glass. Angling the tub lets the bather take advantage of the view. *Builder: Lindal Cedar Homes. Sunroom: Lindal SunRooms. Whirlpool: Jacuzzi. Cabinetry: Beckermann.*

BUILT-IN FEATURES

Natural light streams down through a window in the stepped-up ceiling (right). Marble shelves and a platform around the tub add display space. *Designer: Doris Amsterdam/NKBA Design Competition.*

DELUXE SHOWER

Step in for the ultimate showering experience (right). An overhead shower and handheld spray are among the features. Step out, grab a warm towel, and dry off on the built-in bench. *Designer: Design Concepts Plus/Merrie Fredericks, CKD, CBD. Shower: Grohe. Fittings: Harden. Cabinets: Brubaker Kitchens. Sinks, countertop: DuPont Corian. Tile: Walker Zanger.*

THE POWER OF COLOR

There's nothing like color to dress up and personalize a bath. From its bright decor and symmetrical layout, this bath is one of a kind. The well-planned design boasts an array of special features in addition to the essentials.

Taking advantage of a wide-open space, the designers opted for a centrally located whirlpool/dual vanity combination. Located behind the island, a toilet and bidet become artlike fixtures backed by bold laminates. To the right, there's a stacked washer and dryer for added convenience. The shower is a soothing retreat for those who prefer things a little more subtle in the morning hours.

EXTRA STORAGE

Who wouldn't welcome a wall of closets (below) in the master bath? Inside, a special system keeps "his" and "her" wardrobes organized and separate. Closets: Clairson International/Closet Maid.

DELUXE WHIRLPOOL

A detachable spray makes rinsing off easy in this roomy whirlpool (left), backed by colorful storage. Bright colors framing the toilet and bidet add appeal. *Whirlpool, toilet, bidet, fittings: American Standard.*

VANITY FOR TWO

Back-to-back mirrors (right) act as a divider for the double vanity. Colorful panels of laminate cleverly disguise the cabinets. *Designers: Leo Kelsey, CBD, CKD, and Sachi Kemeta. Countertop, laminate: Wilsonart. Sinks, faucets: American Standard.*

LAUNDRY AREA

The curved countertop (far right) becomes a sorting and folding area for towels before they're put away in the cabinets below. Fitting a stacked washer/dryer in a master bath makes good sense. *Washer/dryer: Maytag.*

SUITE OF GLASS

Here's a real getaway—one you don't even have to leave home for. Reminiscent of a Roman bathhouse, this master suite offers all the extras. A vanity for two provides ample room for storage and pampering. The shower, complete with steam, includes a handheld spray and bench. But for those who like lingering soaks, the whirlpool tub is the place to be.

The design is a mix of marble and glass. There's marble on the floor, countertops, and walls. Glass and glass block are used throughout, keeping this spacious bath wide open. Floor-to-ceiling glass-block walls surround the toilet area, creating a semiprivate room.

A more modern look is introduced by the glossy white cabinetry. Black marble on the countertops provides a striking contrast.

AT-HOME SPA

Marble and glass team up in this luxurious steam shower (below), complete with bench and handheld showerhead. Glass gives the master bath a very open feel. Designer: Stephanie Gisoldi/NKBA Design Competition 1993. Shower: Ketcham. Steam shower: Steamist. Fittings: Hansgrohe. Whirlpool: Spas Plus Spa.

VANITY FOR TWO

Two sinks make side-by-side grooming simple (left). The furniturelike vanity has a striking marble top, contemporary white cabinets, large mirror, and built-in lighting. Cabinets: Allmilmo. Sinks: Kohler.

ADDING SOME PERSONALITY

A bath doesn't have to be massive in size and filled with elaborate decoration to make a statement. In fact, bathrooms are often more charming when simple updating is done. Doing something a little different, as the homeowners of these baths did, is the key to an inviting design.

The light decor opens up both baths, although one of them also benefits from a wall of windows. Rounding the sink areas is aesthetically pleasing and very functional. The tubs are rather classic, but updated with black trim.

Tile plays a big role in both bathrooms. In the larger bath, diagonal rows of diamonds dress up the floor. The pattern of black-and-white checkerboard is a bold addition to the other.

PERSONAL TOUCH

The names of this bath's users are set in a taxicablike tile stripe (below). The playful color scheme updates the bath, while adding a whimsical element. *Designer: Joan Halperin.*

SPACE-SAVING IDEA

The semicircular vanity (right) offers a large sink, counter space, and hideaway storage, without taking up too much room. Windows and a raised ceiling open up the bath. *Architect: Austin Patterson Associates.*

PATTERN OF DISTINCTION

A separate tub and a walk-in shower (left) are an easy fit in this spacious corridor layout. Tile patterns cover most of the surfaces and complement the handmade quilt. Design, tile: Terra Designs.

Custom tilework brings a twist of old and new to this *au courant* bath. The colors are softly muted, giving them an antique feel. From the quilt hung gracefully above the tub to the framed mirror and artwork, the bath is filled with time-honored pieces. But the intricate tile patterns of blue, yellow, and white make an up-to-date splash.

The roomy bath is arranged with fixtures along one wall and enough towel bars for the whole family on the other. There's a shower for everyday use and a tub for more leisurely pursuits. Pretty wall-mounted light fixtures and some recessed lighting make the bath bright even at nighttime.

There's a sink for cleansing, cabinets and drawers for storage, and a mirror to take it all in (left). The color-coordinated space is pleasant and personal.

MASTERING A HIGH-RISE

Renovating condominiums poses a special challenge, primarily because building restrictions limit what can be done. This master bath more than passes the test. There's no need to add space here, just a creative rethinking of existing space.

The bath, located in a condominium complex, was made larger by borrowing space from the hallway and repositioning doors. This enabled the designer to add "his" and "her" closets. Two custom vanities, set back-to-back and divided by a large mirror, give the husband and wife grooming areas to call their own.

Mixing marble with mirror makes this bath regal and bright. White macedonia marble is used to create a beautiful whirlpool-tub surround. The glass-enclosed shower includes a built-in seat.

DECORATIVE STORAGE

A double tier of marble-tile shelves (left) is suitable for storing towels and displaying collectibles. The mirrored wall is a glamorous backdrop for the whirlpool. Designers: Tammy Kaplan and Roslyn Kaplan, Associate ASID.

DUAL VANITIES

Backing vanities (right) allow a husband and wife to groom simultaneously and share pleasantries, yet stay out of each other's way. White marble makes the bath appear more spacious. Tile, vanities: Amaru Tile. Fixtures: American Standard.

CELEBRATING COLOR

Vibrant colors turn these three baths into refreshing places you'll want to spend time in. Although they're rather typical in size, their designs are one of a kind.

Aqua sets a tranquil tone in one bath. Tile borders in seaside shades dress up the tub exterior and walls. White fixtures are a clean contrast. To maximize space, the designer opted for a tub/shower combination and a pedestal sink.

High-energy colors create a welcome mat of vinyl in the second bath. The bold countertop easily wipes clean, making it ideal for family use. With a separate room for the toilet, the bath can be used by more than one person at the same time.

The fixtures and vanity may be white, but the third design is dressed with color. Decorative accessories make the space bright and cheery. The large vanity brings in ample storage and counter space.

SMALL SPACE

Teal tile (above) makes this bath roomy and bright. The pedestal sink and tub/shower combination make sense in the limited amount of space.
Designer: John A. Buscarello, ASID. Sink: American Standard. Tile: Hastings.

FAMILY BATH

High-energy colors, like those on this resilient floor (left), are suitable for users of all ages. A door keeps the toilet private. Floor: Armstrong.

SPACIOUS VANITY

Base cabinets and a long run of countertop (left) get together to create a large grooming and storage area. Bright accents make a friendly statement in this contemporary bath. *Stylist: Susan Andrews. Wallcoverings: F. Schumacher.*

Eliminating base cabinets creates a less-confining walkway (right) through this corridor bath. Glass doors on the shower and a private toilet area create the illusion of more space. Floor tile: Dal-Tile.

BIG THINGS IN A SMALL PACKAGE

Looks can be deceiving. This bath measures just six feet by seven feet. And although the space here is limited, the look is anything but small. Marbleized tile on the floors and walls makes the bath plush and bright. A see-through shower door keeps the bath design open. Even the private area for the toilet, at the far end of the bath, is closed off with glass.

The vanity is a little different, consisting of a floating solid-surfacing counter. Rather than using base cabinets, the designer customized the area. Three side-by-side medicine cabinets provide enough storage for everyday necessities. Hidden away behind a movable wall tile, a small compartment houses a hair dryer. Additional storage space can be found near the toilet.

SHOWER DELUXE

Handy built-in compartments (above) offer easy access when showering. The corner seat and detachable rinse spray are added conveniences. *Designer: Carolyn Thomas, ASID, Town & Country Baths. Fittings: Dornbracht. Shower enclosure: Duschqueen.*

HIDDEN FEATURES

Three mirrored cabinets (right) keep the double vanity free of clutter, while a recessed cubicle is disguised behind a wall tile. The detachable spray is a nice faucet feature. *Countertop: DuPont Corian.*

NATURAL LIGHT

A large window (right) brightens the bathing area and offers a great view of the outdoors. The white whirlpool looks crisp in the watercolor-tile platform.
Ceramic tile: Floor Gres Ceramiche. Whirlpool: American Standard.

A SOFTER SIDE OF TILE

This contemporary bath shows why tile is an ideal surfacing material when you want something a little different. The design possibilities are endless. An array of tile shapes, patterns, colors, and sizes are showcased in this bath. The mix-and-match tilework is a nice touch.

Designing this all-tile bath took skill and painstaking planning. The vanity is built into a small nook. Matching door hardware is used on cabinet fronts. A colorful platform, designed to make getting in and out of the deep tub easier, houses a white whirlpool. The all-white fixtures complement the light shades of tile.

PERSONAL TOUCH

A diamond-and-dotlike design (above) runs the length of the tub platform. The same colors are picked up elsewhere in the bath. Fittings: Moen.

BUILT-IN VANITY

Set in a small alcove, this grooming area (left) is surrounded by tile. The decorative patterns blend small squares, triangles, rectangles, and large squares. Tile designers: Jonna Avella Graphic Design and TSI Development.

SHADES OF BLUE

A rather simple bath is turned into a showstopper with tile. With only one window, this space could have been dark. But color-coordinated patterns add a breath of fresh air to the primarily white bath.

The continuity of the tile designs is what's most striking. Rows of diamonds fill the main floor, staying in line right into the glass-enclosed shower. Two rows of flowerlike creations run along the entire perimeter.

The dual vanity works for family members who need to get ready at the same time. The white oval sinks are an interesting contrast to the bright square tiles. The result is a wide-open design. Privacy is guaranteed, though; for those who want a long, relaxing soak—the whirlpool is set in a semiprivate platform.

TILE TERRIFIC

The ceramic patterns in this bath (left) don't miss a beat, continuing right into the shower. Side-by-side grooming is afforded plenty of room at the vanity. Tile: American Olean.

SMALL SPACE

A partial wall (above) lets the bather get away from it all, at least temporarily. Recessed nooks put pretty vases on display. Architect/ designer: Bahamon Dingman.

IN THE LAP OF LUXURY

It's the finishing touches—and everything in between—that make this bath so extraordinary. Set under a vaulted ceiling, the up-to-date design offers everything a couple could need in their master-bath suite.

Built-in vanities at both ends of the bath offer a sink, mirror, hidden hamper, and storage space for "him" and "her." Linen closets, on angled walls opposite each vanity, keep additional supplies accessible yet out of view.

Brecia Oniciatta marble is used throughout this luxurious bath. Other smaller details also make a big impact. Walls are finished and topped with decorative crown molding. Painted florals add a bit of color to the creamy bath.

DELUXE SHOWER

Step into this spacious marble-and-glass steam shower (above) for a dose of relaxation. The marble trim creates a more formal entry. Fittings: Moen.

EXTRA STORAGE

Topped with a marble counter and triple mirror, this built-in vanity (left) offers cabinets and drawers for lots of bathing essentials. Cabinets: Heritage Custom Cabinets. Sink: American Standard.

PLATFORM TUB

Set in a marble surround, this whirlpool (left) offers bathers a look at the Atlantic Ocean, while the view inside is soft and soothing. *Architect: Doreve Nicholaeff. Designer: Thomas F. Leckstrom, CKD.*

Raising the whirlpool to window level (right) lets the bather get a look outside while enjoying a long, relaxing soak. A grab bar (not shown) makes getting in and out of the tub easier and safer. Tile: Dal-Tile.

MODERN AND CLASSIC MIX

Teaming black with white, then adding some gold accents, has a striking result in this master bath. The generous space offers amenities galore, ranging from "his" and "her" vanities to the raised whirlpool.

Each of the two vanities has a white countertop and sink set above high-gloss black cabinets. The tub and its raised platform reverse this color scheme. Here, the black oval whirlpool rests above a base of white. Fittings at the sinks, whirlpool, and shower are black onyx with gold detailing. These and other gold accents throughout the room add to its neoclassic look.

The decor has a natural ambience, with plenty of natural light to let the plants thrive. Black striping adds interest to the floor and whirlpool area. Walls throughout are white, except in the basically black shower.

MAKEUP AREA

An ideal spot (above) for putting on lipstick and such is created with a lowered countertop, oversize mirror, and comfortable seat.
Designer: Janine Jordan, CKD, IIDA.

'HIS' VANITY

A separate grooming area (right) for the man of the house fits snugly into this small alcove. Extra storage space can be found in the narrow white wall cabinet. Countertop: Wilsonart. Fixtures, fittings: Eljer.

PRIVATE QUARTERS

The toilet and bidet (far right) are set apart in their own space. Inside the shower, three walls of black tile play up the room's contrasting color decor. Towel warmer: Myson.

DEPARTURES FROM THE ORDINARY

Nothing brings a sense of elegance to a bath like jewel tones. Their rich appeal can turn an interesting layout into the ultimate retreat. These two highly personalized designs have Eastern influences.

The bath on this page blends complementary dark tones with lighter highlights. White fixtures and a stop-and-go border on the wall offer dramatic contrast. Carefully placed mirrors make the bath bigger and brighter. The result is bold, yet not intimidating.

The second bath is a little bit lighter and more playful. It mixes a variety of colors and shapes with a furniturelike vanity. A round mirror hangs above the oval white sink. The painted ceiling adds subtle tones to the whole bathroom. Although space is limited, all the necessities fit right in. Angling the shower helps maximize space.

VANITY FOR TWO

Black cabinets topped with a jewel-tone countertop (above) make up the furniturelike vanity. A pair of sinks allows for side-by-side grooming.

LUXURY TUB

This contoured whirlpool (right) sits under a trio of windows. Shades allow for better control of light and privacy. Designer: Susan Andrews.

SMALL SPACE

Mixing light and dark (right) makes for an interesting blend that takes the focus away from the size of this bath. The neoangle shower creates a place for the toilet and a dramatic vanity. Designer: Susan Andrews.

MASTER-BATH MAKEOVER

Turning a powder room, a closet, and a full bath into one space was part of the major renovation that created this opulent master suite. By raising part of the ceiling and adding a light soffit, the bath was made even grander.

Limestone, in a subtle shade of rose, is a primary component of the bath. It's found on countertops, floor, tub surround, and shower. Art and beautiful crystal perfume bottles displayed throughout add to the room's airy decor.

This bath has it all. There's a wall-to-wall vanity with two sinks, a large steam shower, a private space for the toilet, and a whirlpool. Glass display shelves at one end of the whirlpool and an all-glass shower enclosure help keep the design flowing. A pocket door separates the bath from the adjoining master bedroom, creating one huge suite.

COUNTER APPEAL

Limestone lends a soft touch to the vanity countertops (above). The dropped counter creates a sit-down makeup area. *Sinks: Kohler. Faucets: American Standard.*

VANITY FOR TWO

This wall-to-wall vanity (left) includes "his" and "her" sinks and generous storage space. The master bath overlooks the couple's garden. *Designer: Marlise Karlin Designs.*

AT-HOME SPA

Body-soothing amenities, like the glass steam shower and whirlpool tub (left), turn this bath into a tranquil retreat. *Shower: Steamist. Whirlpool: Kohler.*

A COUPLE OF GEMS

Interesting layouts, upscale products, and diamond accents make these two baths sparkle.

A magnificent view takes on murallike proportions in the first bath. "His" and "her" vanities run along two facing mirrored walls. Natural cabinets are highlighted with a black-tile countertop. Tile borders in black bring some sizzle to the walls and the tub platform.

The second bath is an ideal place for pampering. Without being pretentious, it offers a slew of luxuries. There's an extended vanity, a platform tub, and a detached makeup area. The package is tied together by teal tile used on the lower half of the bath. Fixtures were selected to match.

In the plush bath below, windows and a skylight bring the outside in. Two furniturelike vanities create personal space for the couple of the house. Designer: Lindal Cedar Homes.

Teal tile and fixtures (right) add delightful accents to this white master bath. Recessed shelves keep towels handy, while the detached makeup area is a nice finishing touch. Fixtures: Eljer. Tile: American Olean.

ROOM WITH A VIEW

If you have a great view, enjoy it. This master bath takes advantage of its lakefront address. One oversize window, set above the whirlpool, lets the sun stream in. Two sliding glass doors allow you to step onto a porch for a better look, while keeping the room bright with natural light.

The basically all-white bath is tastefully done. The extended vanity makes great use of a long expanse of wall space. At the bath's far end, a makeup area offers an appropriate lighting and mirror combination. Angled above, the television can be watched from several locations, including the tub. Base cabinets are ideal for keeping grooming necessities and towels close by.

Pretty little extras, like the flowers set in the tub surround and the throw rug, add colorful accents. A wall of glass block sets the toilet apart from the rest of the room.

LIGHT & WHITE

This tranquil bathing area (below) blends marble, glass, and glass block. Colorful plants bring a touch of the outside indoors. Designers: Stephanie Harrington-O'Neill and Timothy Patrick.

WALK-OUT PATIO

Sliding glass doors (left) visually expand the space, while giving access to an outdoor patio. For indoor enthusiasts, a television is angled above the vanity. Architect: Robert Wine, AIA.

STORAGE AT ITS FINEST

VANITY FOR TWO

Black sinks, limestone countertops, and natural redwood cabinetry may contrast, but they work nicely together in this dual vanity (below). Custom cabinets provide storage galore and a classy appeal. Designers: Shelley Patterson and Linder Jones/NKBA Design Competition 1992. Fixtures: Kohler. Fittings: Grohe.

For years now, the built-in look has been popular for bath cabinets. Vanities blend with the walls. Medicine cabinets are recessed. Although colors, materials, shapes, and sizes may vary, there's a common thread among many bath vanities and storage areas.

The bath showcased here is a little different. This California beauty includes custom cabinets that have a furniturelike quality. Take a close look at the vanity mirrors, for example. On the opposite wall, a freestanding unit with glass doors and open shelves keeps towels dry.

The narrow bath opens up with a raised ceiling and two skylights. A trio of windows around the tub platform makes the space even brighter.

NARROW SPACE

An eight-foot-square addition (above) created a spot for the whirlpool tub and three surrounding windows. Tub: Paradise.

LET THE SUN SHINE IN

No other product opens up a bath better than glass. If you plan carefully, you can use glass in ways and places that you may never have thought of. These two sunny bathrooms are perfect examples.

The shower in the bath on this page offers an interesting twist: a frameless glass door. By eliminating the fourth shower wall, the designer was able to extend the tub platform and create a convenient seat. Sand tones keep this modern bath simple and inviting. The dual vanity is up to date, while the whirlpool and accompanying platform are classics.

The second bath offers front-row seats to the homeowners' magnificent garden. In fact, the shower and bathroom open onto the family's courtyard. Light colors used throughout keep the focus on the outdoor surroundings. A small room with a door creates a private toilet area.

LUXURY SHOWER

Floor-to-ceiling glass shower doors (below) keep the view wide open. The double vanity offers one side for "him" and one for "her." Designer: Ann M. Schwalm/NKBA Design Competition 1992. Sinks: Kohler. Fittings: Altmans. Cabinets: Wood-Mode. Countertops: Nevamar.

WALLS OF GLASS

A creative design makes it seem as if the shower is outside rather than in (right). The luxury bath is drenched with desert sunlight. Designer: Timothy Huber/NKBA Design Competition 1992.

PLAYING UP COLOR

Festive mosaic bands are a warm welcome to this white and airy master bath. But don't be fooled by the tile's lighthearted look. This bath is hardworking—and it's packed with all the extras.

For starters, there's the flowing layout that incorporates "his" and "her" vanities with ceiling-high mirrors and pullout hampers. There's even a full-size linen closet and a private place for the toilet and bidet.

The design wouldn't be complete without the whirlpool and shower. And what a shower it is! Inside are seven sprays for all-over cleansing. Temperature-control valves prevent water from getting too hot. The shower pan and entire ceramic floor are kept warm by an in-floor hydronic heating system.

ON THE FLOOR

Decorative bursts of color dress up white tile (left). What you can't see, though, is a built-in heating system that keeps the floor warm to the touch. Designer: Van-Martin Rowe. Tile: Ann Sacks Tile and Stone. Sink: Kohler.

ULTIMATE SHOWER

Two warmers outside the shower (right) keep towels cozy, dry, and within reach. Inside, there are seven head and body sprays for a total body experience. Towel warmers: Myson. Showerheads: Hansgrohe.

PRIVATE QUARTERS

Six different types of glass block create a semiprivate alcove for the whirlpool (above). The wide ledge simplifies getting in and out of the tub. Glass block: Pittsburgh Corning. Tub: American Standard.

CLEAN SLATE

With a backdrop of green slate, this bath mixes the old and the new. The floor and wall tiles are ageless, bringing a classic appeal to the oversize master bath. Stone and other natural materials are very popular in today's bath designs.

The separate vanities are contemporary. Here, the rounded sink area is mimicked above by the light valance. This adds an interesting detail and puts lighting right where it's needed most for the person applying makeup or washing up at the sink.

The most dramatic part of the bathroom is the whirlpool tub. It has its own private room, separated from the main part of the bath by double doors. To make the space seem even larger, mirrors have been placed at both ends of the tub platform.

MASTER TOUCHES

Individual vanities (left) let communication flow between their two users, but storage and grooming are kept separate. Designer: Kenneth Neumann, FAIA. Sinks: Kohler. Fittings: Jado.

LUXURY WHIRLPOOL

If there's space, why not create a separate room (right) for lingering soaks? With the double doors shut, privacy is guaranteed. Tub: Kohler. Slate: Virginia Tile Company.

SHOWER DELUXE

Individual controls (above) help adjust water flow and temperature for the showerhead and body spray. An etched design dresses up the glass shower door. Fittings: Kallista.

EVERYDAY LUXURY

The ideal combination in a bath is a functional plan with a pleasing design filled with fresh ideas. Of course, much of this is subject to personal taste and priorities. But that's what makes planning a new bath so interesting.

This beautiful bath shows that elegance can be warm and inviting. Taking advantage of natural light, the decor is bright and cheery. Generous counter space and storage are practical features of the lovely double vanity. Centering the makeup area puts the sinks just a step away. Additional lighting and a cushioned seat make the space more comfortable both day and night.

Other finishing touches, from the decorative window treatments to the etched shower enclosure, turn this bath into a cozy retreat.

SIT-DOWN VANITY

A cushioned seat, ample lighting, and a central location keep the makeup area (left) accessible and user-friendly. Designer: Carol Fox, ASID.

A DOUBLE VIEW

Bathers can relax by enjoying the outdoor scenery or their favorite television show (right). The set can be watched from several locations in the bath by moving the TV tray. Fixtures: Kallista.

MARBLE AND MAHOGANY

W hat bathroom doesn't benefit from an abundance of natural light? This California bath is no exception. Angled windows along an entire wall are dramatic and practical. But there are other eye-catching features.

The large shower has a space unto itself. By using a glass enclosure, the designer was able to continue the room's flow of wood and marble. Curving a pair of vanities along the walls maximizes space. Topped with gray marble, the vanities are filled with cabinets for hiding away bathing essentials.

This opulent bath features gray marble and mahogany wood throughout—a winning combination.

DESIGN FLOW

With help from the glass shower doors (below), the design in this master bath remains uninterrupted. The row of windows and the marble platform continue into the shower. *Shower enclosure: Shower Lux.*

DOUBLE GROOMING

By customizing a pair of vanities (right) to fit along the curved walls, the designer kept the floor free-flowing. Gray marble and deep mahogany wood are well-suited for this Pacific Coast bath. *Designer: Wayne Walega, CKD/NKBA Design Competition 1991.*

WEST COAST TREASURE

With its gentle curves and glamorous look, this California master bath is a showstopper. The design is set by a flowing walkway that leads to a raised whirlpool tub. A dramatic skylight hovers overhead, bringing in plenty of natural light. It also lets evening bathers do some star gazing. Waves etched into surrounding glass add to the bath's pleasant seaside manner.

Two vanities face each other on opposite walls to create a spacious grooming area. The open floor space allows for more than one person to freshen up at the same time. Countertops are natural marble. A pretty seashell in glass helps divide the room, but allows light to filter through.

TWO VANITIES

Like the waves depicted on the glass within, this layout (left) flows. One vanity gently wraps along the wall, while the other is neatly angled.

PLATFORM TUB

Creative marble shapes and detailing (right) add interest to the whirlpool platform. A background of glass block lets light shine through.
Designer: Marsha Broderick.

ELEGANT MARBLE

An undermounted sink and rounded edge (left) make the marble countertop even more luxurious. Colors throughout the bath are soft, adding to its airy appeal.
Sinks: Kohler. Fixtures: Grohe.

Blocks of color and gold detailing surround the white sink above. A rainbow array of dots dresses up the white-tile counter. Designer: Janet Sperber. Countertop: Southwestern Ceramic Tile and Marble Company. Dots: American Olean.

HIGH ENERGY IN A SMALL SPACE

Although its size may be typical, this master-bath design is one of a kind. The seven-by-nine-foot space fits in all the necessities, including a tub, toilet, vanity, and grooming mirror. But by using bright colors and bold tilework, the designer has given the room a unique personality. The end result takes the emphasis off the size of the room.

The bath is covered with color, from the decorative back-splash/wall border to the tub surround with shiny diamonds. The intricate tile work was carefully planned to complement the homeowner's large collection of folk art. The black-and-white checkerboard accents add another personal touch. (The owner is a professional artist who often uses a similar pattern when working.)

Extra counter space (left) creates a comfortable area for freshening up. Extending the countertop over the toilet is a decorative touch. Rope edging: International Tile. Black-and-white checkerboard: Walker Zanger.

NARROW SPACE

With so many other things to look at (above), you might not notice that this personalized bath is just seven by nine feet. *Base tile: American Olean.*

TILE AS ART

The homeowner's folk-art collection inspired this incredible tile design (left). *Backsplash: Arius Tile.*

TRIP TO THE DESERT

From its sandy mountain backdrop to the colorful cacti and tile work, this bath is the ultimate desert fantasy. Solid surfacing is used throughout to create this playful design.

Separate tiled doorways lead the way to three of the bath's main compartments. There's a shower with an adjustable showerhead in one. In another, a whirlpool tub is filled with some help from a black stallion. Even the toilet has its own space. The main part of the bath features a bench covered in a southwestern fabric. The lavatory is a freestanding mix of wood and solid surfacing.

Not a detail is overlooked. Stucco walls are adorned with a central border that matches the floor tile. Windows are playfully covered with bars for an Old West flavor. Even the mirrors and towels carry out the theme.

DELUXE WHIRLPOOL

Deep in the heart of this bath, a horse-head tub filler (above) adds a light-hearted touch. Scenery was customized using solid surfacing.

FREESTANDING LAV

Topped with a solid-surfacing counter and integral sink (left), this vanity looks like something from the Wild West. The windows, wood-framed mirror, and towels add finishing touches. Solid surfacing: DuPont Corian.

MOOD LIGHTING

Interesting lighting, including a backlit cactus (left), sets the Southwest mood throughout. A built-in seat and recessed storage make showering more comfortable.

BURSTS OF COLOR

The size of this bath may be conventional (right), yet its decor is anything but. By keeping the fixtures a neutral white, the home-owners can easily update or change the room's color scheme. *Designer: Susan Andrews. Tile: Summitville. Paint: Benjamin Moore. Sheet: Fieldcrest.*

HAVING FUN WITH ACCENTS

Whether you decide to go all out or stick to something a little more reserved, nothing breathes life into a bath like interesting details. These two bathrooms may seem quite different—and actually, their look is—but both have a limited amount of space and a southwestern decor to add zest to their designs.

Bold colors grab the spotlight in one of the baths. Cabinets are painted sky blue, while the walls are a deeper shade of blue. Mirrors are surrounded by pink and yellow frames. The white fixtures fit right in. Keeping these neutral makes it easier to change other colors in the room. The tile floor is a checkerboard variation.

The other bath is more subtle, but includes southwestern details nonetheless. A black-and-white checkerboard highlights the mirror. This same pattern adorns the shower walls. Cabinets on the dual vanity are honey colored and finished to look aged. The classic inset panel doors are timeless. The pleated shade and lonestar light fixture are bright extras.

VANITY FOR TWO

Two sinks set in tile (right) make this vanity ideal for a family bath. The lightly stained cabinets lend a casual appeal. Designer: Carol Fox, ASID. Stylist: Donna Pizzi.

PRETTY IN PASTELS

A canopy tub takes center stage in this dreamy bath. Not all bathrooms could house something so large and still fit in all the other appointments. A large bathroom actually creates an additional challenge: keeping the design unified and the fixtures and storage accessible. With careful planning, the designer of this showcase bath has created a cozy space.

With its soft carpeting and colors, this Victorian bath is the ultimate place for pampering. Floor-to-ceiling cabinetry offers an abundance of built-in storage. At the far end, a sit-down vanity is brightened with natural sunlight. Separate sink areas, one for "him" and one for "her," are richly decorated with dramatic mirrors and painted tile and cabinets.

ONE VANITY

Soft florals on the sink and the tile backsplash (above) coordinate with the custom-painted cabinetry. The angled mirror aligns with the sloped ceiling. Fixtures: American Standard.

WHIRLPOOL FOR TWO

A pair of fittings on opposite sides of the tub (right) helps fill this grand whirlpool more quickly. The opulent design includes a chandelier and detailed woodworking. Fittings: American Standard.

MAKEUP AREA

Natural light drenches the sit-down vanity (left). With a complete wall of storage, the homeowners' clothes and bathing essentials are nearby. Designer: Anne Cooper.

DOWN TO THE LAST DETAIL

Design possibilities in bathrooms are endless, but a lot of baths begin with a similar premise. First, there are baths that are neutral. These might pick up colors or patterns used elsewhere in the home. More often, though, they're separate spaces with their own identities. Then, there are baths—like the pretty floral one shown on this page—that are based more on fantasy. You might decide to create a little girl's dream bath, for example. With its painted ribbon floor and latticework, this bath offers a feminine retreat.

The second bath shown here belongs to another category of designs: those that look more like a den or library than a bathroom. Take a closer look at the traditional space. Fixtures are separate, freestanding pieces. The tub surround is cabinetry, rather than tile or marble. An oriental rug, ornate artwork, and mirrors add warmth and personality.

CUSTOM SHOWCASE

Soft florals and custom latticework surrounding the tub (left) are just two highlights of this gardenlike bath. It's all tied together with a pastel ribbon stenciled on the floor. Designer: Julie Boynton. Hand-painted floor: Barbara Sandler. Sink, sconces, toilet roll: Phylrich International. Floral fabric: Stroheim & Romann. Striped fabric: Brunschwig & Fils.

Beautiful carpentry (left) turns the lavatory and tub into pieces of furniture that blend with the finely decorated bath. Recessed open shelving leaves room for dry towels. Wallcoverings: Bob Mitchell Designs.

PERENNIAL BATH BOUQUET

Black and white are often teamed to create a contemporary or country look. However, they can also be used in a design to highlight other colors or provide a striking backdrop for fixtures.

In this Victorian charmer, black and white tiles are softened with light florals. The lower half of the bath is basically black, which adds focal impact to the shapely white pedestal sink.

A row of individual bouquets, including muted shades of green, blue, and gold, sit above the black field. Two blue ladies, on either side of an ornate gold mirror, are painted with complementary colors on three tiles.

To further hold the design together, open shelving is outlined with a matching blue-and-white-dot pattern.

PEDESTAL SINK

Adding a pedestal sink to a bathroom (left) introduces an attractive design element. An added bonus is its space-saving design. Tile: Laufen International.

TWO FOR TWO

Victorian baths come in all shapes and sizes and a variety of colors. White beaded inset cabinet doors give the bath on this page its classic look. Bright florals on the wall bring springtime into the home all year long. This bath includes two separate vanities, added when space was borrowed from existing closets.

Using white makes the bath feel roomier. It also makes cosmetic changes easy. Any wallpaper, accessories, and towels will go with white. A tempered-glass shower enclosure adds to the bath's airy feeling.

Rich cherry wood and marble set the tone in the impressive second bath. A console sink with decorative brass legs greets those who enter. Behind the sink, a partial wall of mirror plays an optical illusion, making the bath appear nearly twice as large as it is. Set further back, a luxurious whirlpool rests in a cherry platform for a built-in look. Additional comforts include a neo-angle shower and a bidet.

EXTRA STORAGE

A tall cabinet (above) makes room for towels and other items the homeowners like to have nearby. A tempered-glass shower door lets light flow through. *Mirrored bath cabinet: Robern. Shower: Grohe. Wallcovering: F. Schumacher and Ralph Lauren.*

TWO VANITIES

Placed opposite each other, two vanities (right) provide individual grooming space. Bright wallcovering, window treatment, and decorative border tiles are inviting touches in this mostly white bathroom. *Designer: Merrie Fredericks/NKBA Design Competition. Cabinets: Brubaker Kitchens. Countertop: DuPont Corian. Tile: Walker Zanger. Toilet: Eljer. Fittings: Harden.*

WOOD APPEAL

With cherry detailing and cabinets and pillars behind the whirlpool (right), this bath has the patrician feel of a bygone era. *Designers: Deborah Schroll and Gordon Schroll/NKBA Design Competition. Cabinets: Crystal. Floor: American Olean. Bidet, lavatory, toilet, whirlpool, fittings: Kohler. Shower door: Ketcham.*

A ROOM WITHIN A ROOM

If you want to add a master bath, but don't want to add onto your home, there's hope. Put the tub and vanity right in the master bedroom. Borrow a closet for the toilet. Or continue to rely on the main family bath for this and the shower. Of course, you'll need enough space for a bed and some furniture.

In this clever design, a corner is transformed into a relaxing retreat. The darker stained cabinets and smoky green countertops blend with the rest of the room. Their furniturelike appeal is perfect for a bedroom. The sit-down vanity and sink are features that most homeowners would welcome in their master bedrooms, with or without the tub. Lighting is intentionally soothing.

MASTER SUITE

A corner of the master bedroom welcomes an extended vanity and built-in whirlpool (left). With its richly stained traditional cabinets and green countertops, the bath fits right in. Designer: Connie Edwards, CKD. Cabinets: American Woodmark.

ALL DRESSED UP

Sometimes it's the little things that make the biggest difference when decorating a bathroom. Take a look at these two beauties. Attractive wall-coverings and fabrics make personal statements. Coordinate these products with tiled walls for greatest impact.

When space and natural light are limited, window treatments can overwhelm a room. Sunlight filters in through a lace curtain in the bath on this page. Soft shades of pink are brought in with the floor tile that extends halfway up the wall. Crown molding acts as a decorative divider between the tile and wallpaper. This is an interesting extra that is being seen frequently in Victorian and traditional baths.

Garden colors and sponge-painted walls give the second small bath a fresh appeal. The valance leaves part of the window exposed to let in daylight, while still dressing it up. Matching stripe and floral fabrics on the shower, sink, window, and chair unify the design.

FREESTANDING PIECES

A creamy pedestal sink (above) with a fluted base is well-suited for a Victorian decor. The corner table and chair are nice finishing touches. *Floor: Country Floors.*

EASY DETAILS

One way to conceal unsightly plumbing is to add a festive skirt (right). Pick a fabric that complements the window treatment and shower curtain for best results. *Designer: Susan Andrews. Fabric: Waverly.*

A TASTEFUL RETREAT

Although this vanilla master bath is narrow, it's big on design ideas. The designer didn't overlook a detail when creating a regal mood throughout.

Burgundy and gold accents add timeless elegance to this Victorian getaway. Gold moiré wallpaper lends a truly regal touch. The vanity, complete with built-in hamper, is a glossy gold-patina laminate. Rows of burgundy tile adorn the vanilla walls and tub surround.

Fabrics in this New Jersey master bath were selected to complement the burgundy borders. Another special bonus is the built-in seat next to the whirlpool. It's a perfect place for someone to dry off or rest while waiting for the tub to fill.

CORRIDOR BATH

The whirlpool and a soft bench (left) are added luxuries along one wall of this bath. The design mixes burgundy, vanilla, and gold tones. Fixtures: American Standard.

TRIPLE MIRROR

Plenty of storage space is found in this luxurious bathroom cabinet (right). The vanity fits into its own nook. Designer: Rona Spiegal, ASID. Mirrored cabinet: Robern. Laminate cabinets: Pionite. Countertop: DuPont Corian. Faucets: Jade.

Green-and-white-striped curtains (right), tied back with large tassels, blend with the natural scenery, as well as with the interior decor. Fabric: Scalamandre.

VISIONS OF THE GARDEN

No other color is as natural as green, the basic color of the great outdoors. But with memories of 1970s avocado, some homeowners have shied away from it. This Victorian-and-traditional mix shows how refreshing green can be. The designer's plan was to create a look reminiscent of years past, when formal gardens surrounded the lavish house.

Stars, swags, and tassels give the room a majestic aura, but the design remains comfortable for everyday use. A sit-down makeup area can double as a desk, suitably set between two large windows.

Gold stars and green-tile diamonds (left) create a glittering effect in this updated Victorian bath. Designer: Gail Green, Limited.

Covering a table with draped fabric and glass (right) provides an ideal vanity. It's soaked with sunlight from the nearby windows. Tile: Hastings Tile & Il Bagno Collection.

CLASSIC APPEAL FOR TODAY

Victorian baths are usually filled with furniturelike cabinetry, if not furniture itself, and delicate floral patterns. Window treatments tend to be more ornate than those found in their contemporary counterparts. Often walls and open shelves show off old photographs and classic art. The look can be very classic, or a little more neutral like the bath shown here.

From its crown molding to the gooseneck tub faucet, this bath enjoys an array of Victorian elements. The pastel checkerboard tile and white cabinetry offer more modern hints. Side-by-side sinks with extra storage space are something many homeowners now want in master baths. By incorporating decorating ideas from yesterday and today, the designer has created a timeless bath.

DOUBLE LAV

Side-by-side sinks (right) are separated by a tall storage cabinet in this two-person vanity. The center cabinet is ideal for towels and bulky essentials. Designer: Connie Edwards, CKD. Cabinets: American Woodmark.

Interesting shapes create a unique and practical makeup area above. The lowered space fits snugly between matching vanities. Fabricator: Noel A. Houze.

Solid surfacing allows for endless custom options, including a decorative countertop edge and seamless sink (right). Solid surfacing: DuPont Corian.

PERFECT FOR PAMPERING

Feminine touches turn this large bathroom into a soothing escape. The design is dramatic without being intimidating.

Large pillars surround the tub and support an interesting canopy. The light floor sparkles with pastel diamonds that complement the colors of the wallpaper and tub surround. A bather can enjoy the view outdoors or the television, neatly tucked into a wall of cabinets.

Grooming space is plentiful for two persons. Angled into the corner, a sit-down makeup area anchors the vanity with sinks on either side. A hanging ceiling fan helps with ventilation and fits in with the design's Victorian charm.

There's storage galore in this wall of built-in cabinets (left), which includes a TV set. The whirlpool is set in a pleasing platform with pink accents. *Designer: Bradley Thorn.*

AGED WITH GRACE

Remodeling an old home has its own set of challenges. In the master bath showcased here, the idea was to freshen up the bath, while keeping the design faithful to the home's traditional architecture. The result is a bath that flows with charm.

Touching up the existing framework, from the dramatic archway into the dressing room to the ornate moldings, was the first step. The sconces and chandelier are original to the house. A shell color scheme is used throughout the bathroom, although the green floor and soft floral wallpaper add refreshing accents.

LUXURY TUB

Neatly wrapped with marble, this tub (right) offers a stately place for bathing. Tie-back curtains and an antique chandelier lend timeless appeal.

GROOMING AREA

An antique dressing table (above) fits right into the classic design, while providing the lady of the house a lovely place for pampering. Designer: Marilee Schempp, ASID/Design I.

DRESSING ROOM

If space permits, an open dressing area (right) is a great addition to the bathroom. Shades of shell highlight the two rooms' moldings and trim. Paint: Benjamin Moore.

HINTS OF THE GREAT OUTDOORS

A mention of natural colors probably doesn't conjure up images of rich greens or reds, or sky blue for that matter. But think a little more about nature. Imagine a fully blossomed garden on a spring day or falling leaves in autumn. The tile used in the bath featured here is quite natural. Teamed with lightly finished cabinets, the colors bring a taste of the outside indoors.

Many interesting options are also found within the bath. Who wouldn't enjoy relaxing on a built-in seat while waiting for the tub to fill? There's even a spot for keeping books safe and dry. The toilet is housed in a private room for convenience. Twin sinks allow side-by-side grooming.

DOUBLE VANITY

There's room for two at this striking vanity (above). Rather than sacrifice a window, the designer used a large framed mirror above one sink and a medicine cabinet alongside the other.

TILE TERRIFIC

Walls of diamonds (left) dress up the shower, while complementing the floor and border tiles. The color scheme has environmental roots.

BUILT-IN BENCH

Whether used as a temporary retreat from a busy household or for waiting while the tub fills, comfortable seating (left) serves many purposes in this bath. Designer: Accent On Design.

ONCE UPON A LOFT

It's no wonder the eye looks up when you enter this pretty bath. The vaulted ceiling with hand-painted beams makes the space even grander. If you're remodeling an attic or building up, take a look at this layout for some design ideas.

Soft shades of green dress up the light decor. Classic raised-panel cabinets in a natural finish work well in many room styles. In this bath, green inset accents and beading along the wall cabinets create an antique look. The extended L-shape vanity is anchored in the corner. On one end is a sit-down makeup area, while the platform tub fits comfortably at the other.

Cabinetry, customized for a perfect fit (right), is packed with drawers and doors for hiding away everything someone could need in a bathroom. Crisp white counters highlight the L-shape. Solid surfacing: DuPont Corian.

PERSONAL TOUCHES

Decorative painting on the beams (right) transforms them from eyesores into design assets. Brass fixtures and decorative tiles, like those behind the tub, offer countless design possibilities.
Designer: Jackie Balint, CKD.

DECORATED WITH TILE

If you look too quickly, you might only notice this bath's blue-and-white color palette. But what's really interesting is the tile patterns and other details that dress up the bath, yet keep it cozy.

The whirlpool tub set in a platform is a modern amenity. But with Colonial blue tile and ornate ceramic floral-and-rope-relief borders, the bathing area retains its classic appeal. On the far end, a half wall creates a private space for the tub. There's room for the toilet and vanity on the other side. Blue-and-white tile holds the design together, as does the hardwood floor.

TILE CREATION

Blue wall tiles (above) suggest a chandelier in the tub area. Behind the tub, a pretty display shelf provides extra storage for towels and the like. Tile: Florida Tile.

AT-HOME SPA

Soaking in a whirlpool (right) is therapeutic for the body and soul. A detachable spray makes rinsing off easier. Fixtures: American Standard.

NATURAL LIGHT

This vanity-for-one (left) is brightened during the day with sunlight. From its antique faucets to the marblesque counter, the look is decidedly traditional.

NATURAL BACKDROP

One of the easiest ways to change the look of a bathroom is to refinish the walls. Selecting new wallcoverings or a fresh coat of paint immediately makes a difference. Tile is another option. You can always go with a solid base and then add a simple row of accent tiles. Some bright or intricate patterns carefully mixed in can make a bolder statement. You can also use the walls for a grand backdrop, as in the bath shown here.

The walls are filled with hints of summertime. Butterflies fly free. Birds sing with color. Bouquets of flowers are in full bloom. Scenes of nature go with any style bath, but teamed with a scalloped sink, ornate fittings, and white fixtures, they create a look that is distinctly traditional.

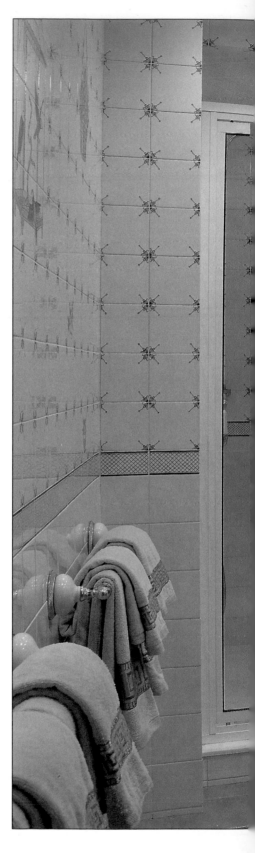

DELUXE VANITY

The scalloped sink and decorative faucet with ceramic inserts (left) are all traditional. The rounded vanity, however, adds a modern element. *Designer: Arthur Barbanell, ASID.*

FINAL DETAILS

Finishing touches, including the matching ceramic and chrome accessories (right), help unify the bath's design. A pale blue stripe runs along the four walls right into the shower. *Tile: Eton.*

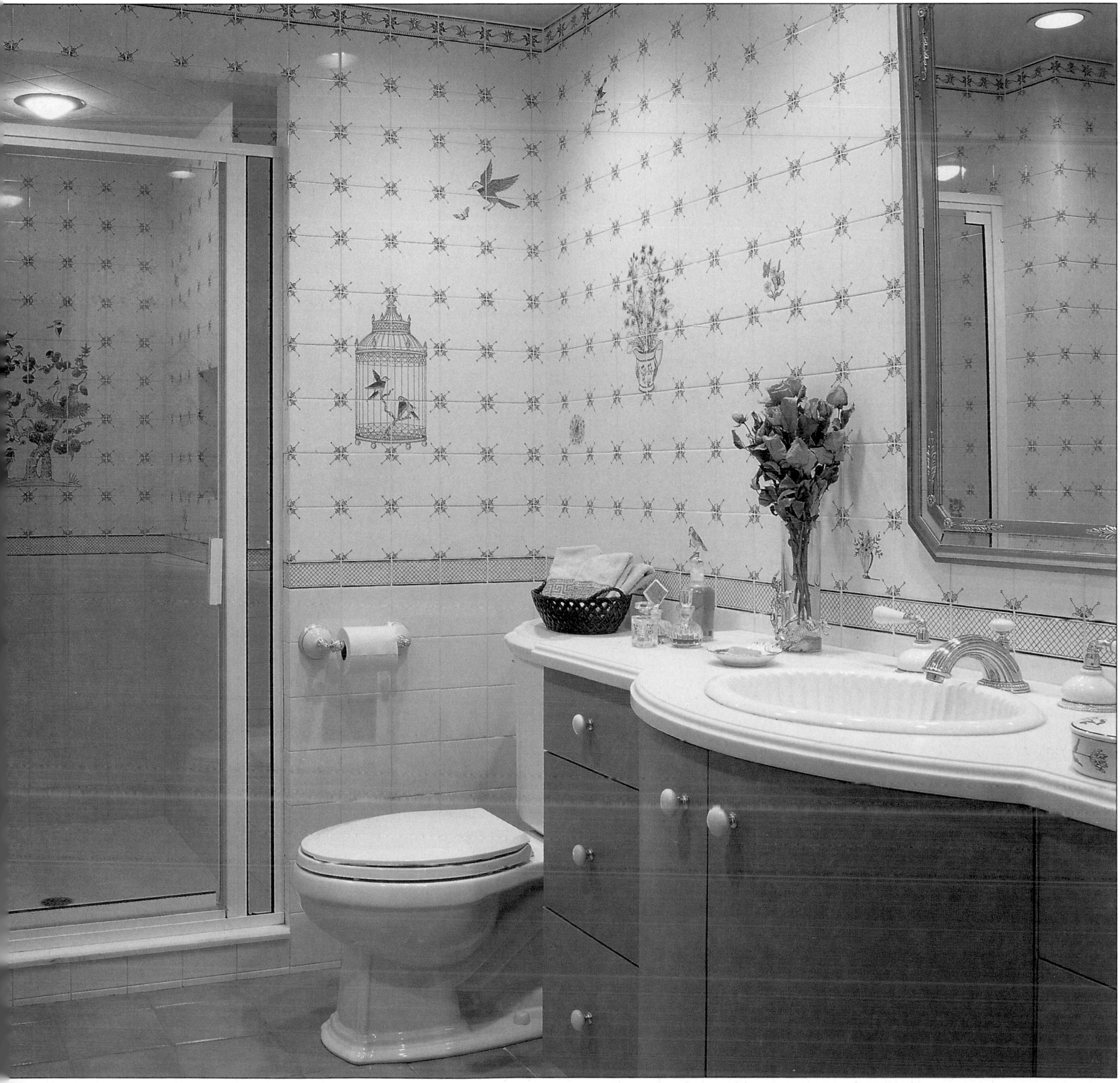

SMALL CHANGES FOR BIG RESULTS

Yellow can work wonders for brightening a room, as the two small bathrooms showcased here demonstrate.

Working around existing yellow fixtures was the challenge in the bath on this page. To make the color scheme a little more subtle, the designers selected a striped fabric for the shower curtain and vanity skirt. The toilet is also draped.

Another challenge—one faced by many homeowners—was to make the decor complement an adjoining bedroom. The bedroom's color scheme of sandy neutrals, hunter green, and yellow is picked up in the hand-painted starfish on the walls.

Small green leaves against a backdrop of yellow-and-white stripes revitalize the other bath. This minimakeover, however, preserves the room's traditional styling. A matching wallpaper border is used at the ceiling. Other classic touches include the gold-framed vanity mirror and candlelight fixtures.

SIMPLE CHANGES

Striped fabric and a hand-painted starfish motif (above) update this yellow bath, while unifying the decor with that of the adjoining bedroom. Designers: Katie Goldfarb, IFDA, and Laura Chandler, IFDA.

QUICK CHANGE

Adding lively window and shower treatments (right) is the first step toward sprucing up a bathroom. Put up a matching decorative wall border, and you've got a whole new look. Designer: Jeffrey Scott Queripel. Fabric: Rose Cummings.

STORAGE ISLAND

The center island (above) has a dual purpose. It provides ample storage, while setting the design and traffic flow. Designer: Absolute Bath Boutique.

LUXURY TUB

An oval whirlpool, complete with headrest (right), sits gracefully in a triangular tile platform. Although the ceramic surface, wallcovering, and fabrics are quite different, they blend together nicely. Tile: Hastings Tile & Il Bagno Collection.

ISLAND MAKES A SPLASH

Islands are popular in kitchens, but they've yet to make it big in baths. Few homeowners could float a center island in their bathroom and still have space left over. The bath featured here easily fits all the luxuries its owners could ever want, including a center island.

Angled in one corner is a large shower. In the other corner, a door separates the toilet from the main part of the bath. The plan provides two vanities, both of which are spacious. The lady of the house can take advantage of "her" sit-down grooming area. "His" vanity provides ample counter space for shaving accessories.

White is used for the basics: cabinets, fixtures, and floor. Color is added with mosaic-tile counters and striped wallpaper. Using different colors, materials, and patterns shows just how effective mixing and matching can be.

PRIVATE QUARTERS

A mirrored door (above) closes off the toilet from the main area. Cabinet storage keeps "her" grooming essentials out of view.

'HIS' VANITY

Separate grooming areas (left) are provided in this light and lively bath. Drawers make necessaries easy to locate. Fixtures, fittings: American Standard.

MASTER-BEDROOM EXTENSION

Some baths just don't look or feel like bathrooms. They remind one more of adjoining bedrooms or nearby living rooms. The result is a warm, refreshing space that lacks any suggestion of a typical task-oriented bath design.

This master suite is a perfect example. It includes all the necessary elements in subtle ways. The color scheme is what you might expect to find elsewhere in the house. Pretty plaid accents offer a friendly touch.

Custom cabinets are used for the lavatory and makeup area and as additional storage. Their arrangements, though, could double as a desk and dresser in any other room of the house.

AT-HOME SPA

Uplifting colors and large windows create a tranquil mood (above) in the corner set aside for the whirlpool tub. Feet on the vanity suggest a bathroom dresser with sink. Fixtures: Kohler.

MAKEUP AREA

Custom touches turn cabinetry into an extraordinary seated grooming space (right). Glass shelves showcase items not typically displayed in a bathroom. Stylist: Susan Andrews.

OPEN LAYOUT

Light colors, playful plaids, and heavy crown molding (right) turn this space into a true master-suite retreat. The spacious plan includes a shower, whirlpool, and two vanities. Designer: Janet Alholm.

CRISP, CLEAN, AND WHITE

Using wall-to-wall cabinets in a bathroom not only increases storage space, but also creates an interesting design statement. Most people let a dramatic whirlpool or decorated walls be the focal point of their baths. Why not let the cabinetry play a bigger role?

In the two English-style baths shown here, white cabinets stray from the familiar built-in look. Customization allowed for planning of every inch of space. The result is plenty of concealed storage and lots of open shelves for decorative displays.

Beautiful grooming areas are a delight to spend time in. While one bath goes for a classic slipper tub, the other has an up-to-date model. However, the surrounding pillars and classic fittings keep the decor strictly traditional.

RECESSED TUB

Custom cabinetry, arched mirrors, and decorative details (left) create elegant surroundings for the tub. The light decor is highlighted by a checkerboard floor. Cabinets: Smallbone.

DOUBLE VANITY

Two sinks (left) bring side-by-side grooming to this well-dressed bath. The space is soaked with natural light. Cabinets: Smallbone.

DOWN TO THE LAST DETAIL

Columns and decorative moldings are often used in large baths to create visual separation between fixtures. They're also used to spruce up a space with classic charm. But rarely do the architectural details tie together every inch of the design as those in this bathroom do.

A large vanity sits front and center. One of the room's many focal points, the freestanding piece is more like art than furniture. It mixes rustic and gold tones with ornate decoration that you'd expect to see in an ancient Roman structure. An additional place for pampering is found at the glamorous sit-down makeup area.

The variety of oversize shapes used in the design is also interesting. The vanity has a triangular top above a large oval mirror and two rectangular columns of sorts. Above the tub rests a massive rectangular window set in an even larger circle.

DELUXE WHIRLPOOL

Contoured backrests make relaxing in the jetted tub (above) even more comfortable. Tile on the platform steps features an embossed design. *Tub: Hydro Systems. Fittings: Dornbracht. Embossed tile: Country Floors.*

CENTER VANITY

This grand vanity (right) and other open surfaces are the ideal setting for the homeowners' art collection. Architectural details turn typical bath fixtures into art themselves. *Designer: Schaerer Design.*

TASK ORIENTED

There's enough room to divide the bath according to function. The makeup vanity (right) has its own spot along the wall. Back-to-back sinks are centrally located. *Sinks: Kohler.*

VIEW FROM ABOVE

Large windows allow the sun to shine in. The only problem is positioning and dressing them to keep nosy neighbors out. If the bath is out of viewing range, you don't have to worry. If it's not, you can still go for glass. Just select treatments that give you the greatest control over light and privacy.

The bathroom shown here is secluded enough so that the window can be virtually bare. Curving cabinetry adds to the bath's lovely, free-flowing layout. The custom design is also practical. A curved corner provides a safe and roomy spot for the lavatory, in addition to space for a sit-down grooming area.

Striped wallcovering and fabric play up the sunlit decor. Pretty extras, like the chandelier and built-in planter, give the bath its finished look. Cabinet doors and faucets combine crystal with polished gold and brass.

EXTRA STORAGE

Interesting curves and angles (below) create a one-of-a-kind extended vanity with plenty of space to store all necessities. Doorknobs are a mix of crystal and gold.
Cabinets: Brubaker Kitchens. Cabinet hardware: Esquema. Sink: American Standard.

MARBLE DELIGHT

Peach, beige, and white (left) blend together in this bath's beautiful marble tub surround and countertops. The floor is a combination of white, rose, and pearl.
Designers: Merrie Fredericks, CBD, CKD, and Philip Fredericks/NKBA Design Competition 1994. Whirlpool: Americh. Whirlpool fixtures: Phylrich.

FIRST-RATE MIX

You might not expect to find wood beams in an opulent, natural-stone bath. The combination, however, makes perfect sense. Stone and wood go hand in hand in nature. Also, most people think nothing of topping wood cabinets with a granite or marble countertop, if their budget permits.

In this bath, the wood-plank ceiling makes the bath more rustic. It's the whirlpool tub, though, that grabs immediate attention. Backed by natural light, the whirlpool is set in a user-friendly platform. The wide ledge makes getting in and out of the tub much easier. Vanities on either side are identical twins. Richly colored carpeting adds to the room's plush atmosphere.

EXTRA STORAGE

Glass-front cabinets (left) showcase collectibles while keeping them safe and dry. The furniturelike design complements the bath vanities. Designer: Kathleen Donohue, CKD, CBD/NKBA Design Competition 1994.

TRIPLE LUXURY

Drenched in sunlight, the ornate whirlpool (right) is ideal for refreshing soaks. Separate vanities allow two people to groom simultaneously without getting in each other's way.

COLORFUL ACCENTS

Little bursts of sunshine brighten this dual vanity (right), which is highly stylized with architectural details. Designer: Arthur Barbanell, ASID. Marble: Fuda. Fixtures: Sherle Wagner.

CHANGING ROLE OF VANITIES

Think back to bathrooms of the 1970s. The vanity usually consisted of a sink and laminate counter. A simple medicine cabinet provided a mirror and limited storage. Two doors opened to the area directly under the sink. Narrow drawers were sometimes added, along with a small cutout that could have been used for a stool but usually wasn't.

Times have changed, and so have vanities. Today's vanities offer more storage and counter space in a customized package. They aren't necessarily bigger. They're more efficiently planned. Take a look at these two bathrooms' vanities. Both are of beautifully painted wood and dressed up with pretty hardware. One features an angled makeup area. The other fits in a second sink and a tall cabinet for towels.

SPACE SAVER

Angling the whirlpool and makeup area (below) maximizes space in this master bath. The shower and a second vanity fit on the opposite wall. Cabinets: Dura Supreme.

LIFE'S LITTLE LUXURIES

PRIVATE QUARTERS

The platform tub (below) may be out in the open, but the toilet is tucked away in its own little nook. Tub: American Standard. Faucets: The Broadway Collection. Toilet: Kohler.

Plenty of light. Extra storage. Privacy. These are just a few of the things homeowners often put at the top of their bathroom wish lists. Generally, people want a functional space that also looks great. What's nice is that you don't have to sacrifice one for the other—a point that this bathroom nicely proves.

"His" and "her" vanities provide a lot of cabinet space. The cabinets and countertop here were customized to resemble a finely crafted piece of furniture. Opposite the trio of vanity mirrors, a glass-enclosed shower keeps light flowing through the entire bath. A soffit and crown molding are classic additions.

The old blends with the new in the tub area. An existing cast-iron tub was reglazed and updated with a marble platform. Modern comforts are many. The vanities include a makeup area and individual hampers for dry cleaning and laundry. A floor warmer keeps the marble comfortable on cool days.

VANITY FOR TWO

Separate sinks are a popular feature in bathroom vanities. Crafted of alderwood, the cabinets (right) conceal one hamper for laundry and another for dry cleaning. Designer: Barbara Barton, CBD/NKBA Design Competition 1994. Sinks: Kohler.

GETTING PERSONAL

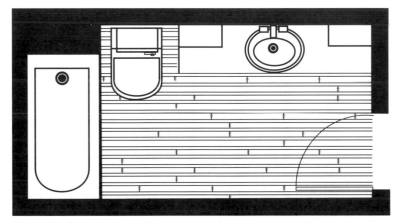

Floor plan for bathroom below.

Baths have begun to warm up in recent years. Designs are more individualized to suit specific needs and lifestyles. Then, too, homeowners are adding items that reflect their own interests and hobbies. These decorative touches can be either obvious or subtle.

Sailing must be something of a passion for the owner of the bath on this page. Take a look at the classic sailing vessel etched in wood above the bookshelf. The wall space behind a toilet is often left empty—here, it's a great place to hang a photograph or piece of art. Adding towels with an appropriate design, like anchors, is a simple way to tie in a hobby.

Even if you stay away from the theme, you can say a lot with the colors you select. Perhaps the rich shades used in the second bath are personal favorites; maybe they pick up where the master bedroom left off. The room's built-in hamper and bench are just what the homeowners wanted. A family photograph on the countertop keeps loved ones nearby.

SHIP AHOY

Subtle decoration, like an etching above the water closet (right), reflect an appreciation of sailing. Even the rich wood is reminiscent of that used in clipper ships. Designers: Merrie Fredericks, CBD, CKD, and Philip Fredericks/NKBA Design Competition 1994.

FREE FROM CLUTTER

From the regal color scheme to the window seating (right), this bath is a reflection of its owners' tastes. The built-in hamper and accessible storage keep the countertop free for displaying a family photograph. Designer: Merrie Fredericks, CBD, CKD.

LIGHT AND DARK CONTRASTS

Dark shades of marble add a rich flavor to these two bathrooms. What makes the deep tones really stand out, though, is the magnificent light backdrops on which they're set. Blending light and dark tones creates a winning combination.

Although the cherry cabinets in the one bath are dark, the tub and shower are white. This contrast is more subtle than a contemporary black-and-white checkerboard bath, but its impact is no less dramatic. Subtle pastels on the walls and in the window fabric add a soft touch of spring. These colors blend with the greenery brought in through the massive tub window.

A unique tub-and-shower combination takes center stage in the other bath. Here, dark glossy marble surrounds a white tub and other fixtures. Decorative pieces, like the rugs and cushioned seats, add uplifting color. Extra storage is provided by the two vanities and tall bureaulike cabinet.

GREAT VIEWS

Bathers in the whirlpool below can enjoy the natural view outside and the warm luxury inside. A separate deluxe shower features a tile bench and recessed storage.
Designer: Kenneth J. Thelen, CKD, AIA. Cabinets: Coosa Valley Cabinets.

SHOWER & TUB

Teaming up glass and dark marble, a dramatic island (right) for the oversize shower and tub steals the show in this opulent bath.
Designer: Sharon Overstake, CKD. Tub: Kohler. Cabinets: Fieldstone.

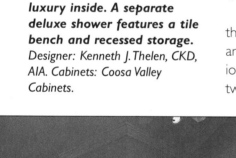

LIGHT AND AIRY RETREAT

There's nothing like sunlight to brighten a bathroom. Designers often suggest that clients add a window or enlarge an existing one when planning a new bath. The only drawback is that windows take away wall space. If space is at a premium, evaluate whether you'd rather have a healthy dose of sunlight, extra storage space, or a separate tub and shower.

The refreshing bathroom showcased here features an attractive window bay. Three walls of windows surround the pretty platform tub. Attractive wood shutters allow the bather to control light and privacy. They also bring in a hint of the orient.

A long expanse of wall houses the extralong double vanity and provides plenty of storage space. Mirrors, framed to blend with the base cabinets, make the bath appear to be nearly twice its size.

BATHING ALCOVE

Set in its own niche, the whirlpool (left) is placed away from the main flow of the bathroom. Shutters keep the space bright yet private. Designer: Craig Patterson & Associates. Stylist: Susan Andrews.

GROOMING SPACE

Lightly finished base cabinets (right) line up in this traditional two-person vanity. Added lighting and mirrors keep the entire length illuminated. Fixtures, fittings: American Standard.

GOLDEN TOUCHES OF ELEGANCE

White has a way of opening up a bathroom and giving it a larger-than-life feeling, especially if the room is big to begin with. Contrasting white with black adds drama to this spacious bath. Its gold accents are like jewelry complementing a splendid evening gown.

The designer paid close attention to architectural details throughout the master bath. Crown and dentil moldings run along the ceiling. Fluted columns and an archway create a formal entry to the whirlpool tub. A similar look is repeated with the vanity mirror. Two angled vanities draw attention to a comfortable makeup area. Other features in the bath include a private space for the toilet and bidet and a glass-enclosed custom-built shower.

DUAL VANITY

Angling the matching vanities (below) adds an interesting design element, while highlighting the makeup area. The all-white vanity is adorned with gold hardware. *Sinks: Kohler. Cabinets: Jay Rambo.*

WHIRLPOOL LUXURY

Set in a formal black-and-white alcove (right), the whirlpool offers a stress-free retreat. The column-and-archway theme is repeated above the vanity. *Designer: Thomas Trzcinski, CKD, CBD/NKBA Design Competition 1993. Tub, fittings: Kohler.*

OPEN TO FRESH IDEAS

As the emphasis on the home continues to grow, more energy is being put into planning bathrooms. Today's bathrooms feature aesthetically pleasing designs and practical amenities. Artwork and crystal treasures fit right into pretty baths. As a result, glass-front cabinets are becoming more and more popular as showcases.

This bathroom features a variety of interesting ideas, both in and out of glass. For starters, there are two large glass-front cabinets that put colorful towels and vases within view. The design flow begins with an angled layout. Separate teal sinks rest on either side of a neoangle cabinet. "His" and "her" vanities are convenient. Putting the toilet in its own small room assures greater comfort.

Mirrors and a 10-foot ceiling create a wide-open feeling throughout. Crown moldings and ornate pillars are consistent with the room's traditional design.

DELUXE WHIRLPOOL

This teal whirlpool tub (left) soothes tired muscles and gives the bather beautiful surroundings to look at.
Whirlpool: Kohler. Fittings: American Standard.

ANGLED PLAN

Two lavatories (left) are separated by kitty-corner base and wall cabinets. The glass-enclosed shower repeats the angular theme.
Designer: Martha Sasso/NKBA Design Competition 1991.
Countertop: DuPont Corian.

ADDING SOME COLOR

Creamy tones are popular in interior design because of their flexibility. Just about anything goes with them. Light colors provide a clean background against which you can easily use accent colors or other interesting details. The two charming baths shown here are good examples.

Just how far you go is up to you. Perhaps a fancy trellis will work wonders in your bath, as it does here. Mustard-and-white wallpaper is refreshing without being overwhelming. A miniprint on the carpet fits right into the traditional scheme.

Stripes also dress up the other bath. The colors used on the shower curtain and sink skirt, both of mattress ticking, are grass green and white. The walls are hand painted with gentle leaves to coordinate with the color scheme.

PERSONAL TOUCHES

With its trompe l'oeil ceiling (left), this creamy bath is tastefully accented with color. The toilet and bidet are placed behind a door for privacy. Designer: Marcello Luzi/Peterson Wicksler Design.

CUSTOM LOOKS

A soft shade of green (right) is introduced with striped fabrics and walls hand painted by the designer. The neutral background makes it easy to change the look of the bath by selecting new fabrics and wallcovering. Designer: Ned Marshall.

ONE BATH BUILT LIKE TWO

If you'd like to remodel a bathroom in your house, but can't figure out how you're going to fit everything you want, it's time to consult a professional. Maybe you'll have to sacrifice a little bit. But a creative expert will probably help you find space in places you'd never thought of.

This award-winning bath was designed for a couple who wanted private areas within the confines of one master bath. Their bedroom had previously included two cramped bathrooms, one for each person.

The designer gave one bath back to the bedroom, while rearranging the other to create a clever design. The final product is more like two separate baths that share a walk-through shower. Each side features a vanity, closet, and toilet. "Her" side also has a platform tub. The peaches-and-cream decor is light and refreshing. Mirrors open up the narrow layout.

'HER' BATHROOM

An angled vanity (below) leaves floor space for the mirrored closet. The sunlit tub is a bathing delight.
Designer: Kathleen Donohue, CKD, CBD/NKBA Design Competition 1993. Sink, tub: Kohler.

PRIVATE QUARTERS

The man of the house also enjoys plenty of storage space (right), a sink for personal grooming, and a toilet on his side of the bath.
Floor: American Olean.

CREATIVE SPACE SAVERS

The center aisle of this pretty white bathroom is nice and roomy. By lining up fixtures on the walls and adding a few angled elements, the designer was able to include everything the homeowners desired.

A large, neoangle shower fits into a back corner. Its glass enclosure keeps the room's design flow uninterrupted, which makes the bath seem longer than it is. A platform around the tub makes getting in and out easier. Just sit on the ledge and swing your legs over.

The vanity features an interesting design. If you look closely, you'll notice that it's actually not as deep as a typical vanity. The sink reaches out into the aisle in an angled countertop that allows enough space for the oval fixture. Matching wood panels on the sink front add continuity. A large cabinet alongside the sink keeps bathing essentials tucked away, yet within reach.

SETUP FOR ONE

Angles lend interest to this narrow vanity (left). The countertop is extended to fit the lavatory, while maximizing aisle space. Designer: Debra K. Ureel/CBI Associates. Architect: Keith A. Logdson, AIA.

SMALL SPACE

Space may be limited, but a little creativity helps get everything in. By angling the shower (right), the designer created a nook for the toilet. Sink, toilet, tub: Kohler. Faucets, shower fittings: Jado. Hardware: Baldwin.

LIGHT AND AIRY LAYOUT

DUAL USE

Storage galore is found in the rosy vanity for two below. The deep drawers are ideal for tucking away bulkier items, such as hairdryers. Designer: Thomas D. Kling, CKD/NKBA Design Competition 1994. Cabinets: Wood-Mode. Sinks, countertop: DuPont Corian. Faucets: Phylrich.

If you're remodeling a small bath and have a nearby closet from which to borrow space, consider the possibilities. Sometimes knocking down a wall or adding a small amount of square footage produces wonderful results.

By eliminating a closet and removing a tub wall, the designer of this bath was able to add a whirlpool tub. And that's not all. The toilet area also has more elbow room. The design is packed with storage. The double vanity offers plenty of counter and cabinet space. Recessed cabinets, like the one above the toilet, are nice features that take advantage of otherwise vacant space.

Rosy hues create a friendly feeling throughout the room. The traditional cabinetry is further decorated with detailed carvings and pink onyx hardware.

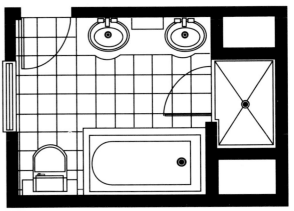

DELUXE SPA

Removing a closet made way for this roomy whirlpool tub (right). Architectural details, including the custom panels on the tub apron, have a classic appeal. Whirlpool, toilet: Kohler.

RAISING THE ROOF

These two baths may seem quite different, but they actually have some design elements in common. Both feature traditional decors with floors having distinctive patterns. Glass lets natural light illuminate the two spaces. And look upward: The raised ceilings, one flat and one cathedral, give these two baths their wide-open feel.

A single star-and-diamond pattern provides a glittering welcome mat in the the bath on the facing page. Marble tones complement the light walls and fixtures. With two pedestal sinks, there's individual space for both "him" and "her." The oversize mirror makes the room appear even grander.

Cherry wood is a classic. The bath on this page neatly contrasts white counters with rich wood tones. On the floor, the green-and-white checkerboard pattern sparkles. The dresserlike vanity is nicely decorated. Finely carved columns create a dramatic entrance.

RICH WOOD

A deep stain on cherry wood (below) gives a timeless look to this airy bath. Designer: Nancy Thornett and Plachter Interior Design. Cabinets: Rutt.

OPEN LAYOUT

Marble gives this spacious bath (left) its elegant look. Twin pedestal sinks serve a functional purpose, while adding shapely design elements. Designer: Accent On Design.

MORE THAN JUST A BATHROOM

Some baths are so pleasant and tastefully done that they are more retreats than rooms. This is one such bathroom.

Rose marble and lightly finished cabinets set a casual yet refined mood. This bath has it all. The shower and the whirlpool tub provide plenty of room for relaxation and serenity. Two vanities keep "his" and "her" grooming separate, yet close enough for enjoyable conversation. The floor is French limestone.

Finishing touches give the bath charm and appeal. A fireplace warms up the space, literally as well as figuratively. Its ornate mantel offers an attractive showplace that would fit just as well in a more formal living room. There's even a television set. Bathers can either watch their favorite shows or take a peak at nature through the window.

Even a spacious bath can be cozy. Rosy tones, light wood, and a fireplace (below) warm up this bath. Designer: Pat K. Robinson, ASID. Architect: Russ Barto, AIA. Cabinets: Trick Shop. Sink: Kohler. Fireplace surround: Raymond E. Enkeboll Designs.

Light cascades through wooden shutters (right) into the tub and surrounding areas. A spacious shower angles at the far end of the bath. One of two vanities is at the other end. Shower enclosure: Century Shower Door. Shower fittings: Grohe, Moen. Tub: Hydro Systems. Tub fittings: Kohler.

BUILT-IN CONVENIENCES

Clutter-free designs are always nicer to look at than their messy counterparts. Clean designs begin with safe walkways and ample storage. Several products are used in a bathroom daily—from toothpaste to makeup to hairdryers. If you don't have cabinets and drawers to store them in, keeping the counters clear can be tricky.

The master bath featured on these two pages uses a lush landscape as its backdrop. Inside, the design is packed with storage amenities—from the dual vanity to separate dressers for undergarments and towels. A pullout hamper encourages users to toss dirty duds out of view, rather than onto the floor.

The look throughout is light and crisp. Mirrors and open shelves keep the design flowing. Sandy limestone on the floor complements the white cabinetry.

HIDDEN HAMPER

Getting damp towels off the floor is made easier with a large pullout hamper (above). The tall cabinet keeps towels dry and within reach of the shower. Designer: Nancy Ruzicka.

AT-HOME SPA

Plush surroundings (left) could make long soaks in this whirlpool tub habit-forming. Shutters can be closed to cover the lower portion of the window, while letting light stream in from above. Stylist: Susan Andrews.

GROOMING AREA

With a large mirror, comfortable seat, and proper lighting, this makeup area (left) is complete. The limestone floor goes nicely with white cabinets.

A LIGHTER SIDE OF COUNTRY

"**C**ountry" has become a buzzword in bathroom and kitchen design in recent years. Many people will react to the mere mention of the style with "love it" or "hate it." But country styling, especially in kitchens and baths, covers a wide spectrum of colors, accents, and products. There are softer looks with a few "country" accents, and there are all-out spaces that include medium wood tones, ornate valances and friezes, open shelving, and a color scheme that you might expect at a down-home picnic.

This black-and-white bath combines country styling with a more contemporary edge. The cabinets, door hardware, and wainscoting are traditional, but the shiny black counters and beautiful medicine cabinet bring the look up to date.

STORAGE SPACE

Louvered doors (left) open to a closet filled with shelves for towels and other linens. Wainscoting on the walls matches the cabinet fronts.

DELUXE VANITY

Plenty of illumination is one feature of the recessed, triple-mirror wall cabinet (right). Drawers in the double vanity pull out for easy access to their contents. Mirrored cabinet: Robern.

SERENE SPACES

This trio of bathing beauties is filled with personal touches that make the rooms warm and cozy for everyday use. Each bath takes advantage of natural light to brighten the already cheery designs. Light wood tones are flexible. They blend right in with a variety of decors.

The first bath on this page includes pastel tile on the walls and a darker shade on the floor. Both colors meet up on the interesting backsplash. An extended vanity allows ample space for two lavatories.

In the second bath, natural greens come inside to create a serene feeling. Cabinets feature a traditional raised-panel design. Surrounded by other appropriate accessories, they're suitable for a country decor.

Shades of blue dress up the bath on the facing page. The wood cabinets finished in light oak contrast the white-paneled tub surround. Accents, including the picket-fence planter, are playful. The vinyl floor is a practical addition—it wipes clean with a damp mop.

BUILT-IN SEAT

A small tile-covered bench (above) fits into its own niche below the undressed window. It's ideal for drying off or waiting for the whirlpool to fill. Designer: Carolyn Haney. Cabinets: Fieldstone.

OPEN SHELVES

One highlight of country baths is exposed storage (right) that puts towels and interesting collectibles in view. Designer: Connie Edwards, CKD. Cabinets: American Woodmark.

SHADES OF BLUE

Blue is a popular color in country designs. This bath (left) nicely contrasts wood tones and colors for a finished look. Designer: Connie Edwards, CKD. Cabinets: Timberlake Cabinet Company.

CHEERY BATHROOMS

Wallcoverings and fabric can work magic in any room. Bright colors in floral and abstract patterns stand out in the two baths showcased here.

The look of a perennial garden is suggested in the small bath on this page. The striped wallpaper is reminiscent of long, hazy summer days. Adding a decorative skirt to the sink is a great way to hide unsightly plumbing. The skirt can be made in a weekend. And if you decide next year that you want a different color or pattern, it's easy enough to change.

The second bath is a real eye-opener. What a way to start the day! The design is basically white with colorful details on the walls, floor, and tub surround. The room glows with sunshine from the skylight above. The luxurious whirlpool tub includes a padded headrest for added comfort during lingering soaks.

SINGLE SINK

Decorative florals drape the sink (left) and walls for a country-garden feel. Collectibles are openly displayed, adding a personal touch. Wallcovering, fabric: Waverly.

NATURAL LIGHT

Sunlight flows freely, thanks to the angled skylight (right). Colorful wallcoverings bring a cheery lift to the white bath. Wallcoverings: Color Tree Designs by Eisenhart.

FIRST-RATE FLASHBACK

A lighthearted design doesn't mean a bath is any less functional. Colorful variations of the classic checkerboard playfully dress up this space. The layout itself lets traffic flow through easily, while keeping things separate enough for comfort. It's got all the extras, too.

A deluxe makeup area sits to one side of the bath's main entrance. Behind it, a false wall separates the toilet from the main part of the bath. This is a pleasant privacy feature. The shower is also designed with privacy in mind.

There's additional grooming space at the blue-topped vanity with a sink. Edges are silver for a total retrospective flavor. The color-coordinated floor matches the countertop while gently contrasting the smaller, softer squares on the walls.

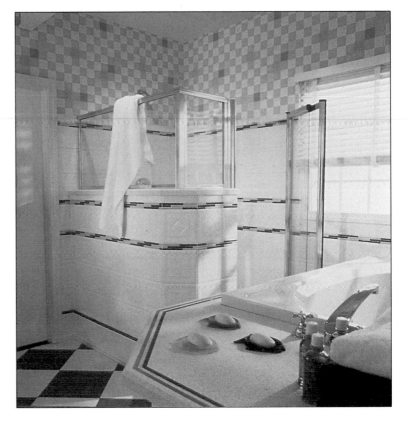

MAKEUP AREA

Lights, camera, action! This glamour vanity (left) is complete with a large mirror, lots of drawer space, and a cushioned seat. Designers: John A. Buscarello, ASID, and Gail C. Olsen, CKD.

SHOWER ROOM

Tile walls and glass (above) create a spacious private shower. On the opposite wall is a whirlpool tub.

DELUXE VANITY

With its bright blue countertop and silver trim (right), this vanity is an eye-catcher. Muted shades add a light touch to the checkerboard walls. Stylist: Pamela Abrahams.

HOOKED ON STYLE

If this bath is any indication, nice things certainly can come in small packages. The designer completed the bath so tastefully that you might overlook its size almost entirely. The vanity is lovely, with a durable marble countertop set on brass legs. Its floating image keeps the floor within view, which helps create the feeling of greater space.

The combination of black and white will never go out of style. In this bath, black is used as a striking accent on white surfaces. The floor features black diamonds contrasting large white squares. Three rows of black tile decorate every wall.

MARBLE VANITY

A slab of marble with an under-mount sink (left) becomes a perfect vanity with the addition of brass legs and a round wall mirror. Mirror: Kohler. Tile: Nemo.

IN THE SHOWER

Any shower can be made a little more convenient with a hand-held spray for rinsing (right). A partial wall helps keep water off the floor and vanity. Designer: Ferne Goldberg Interior Design.

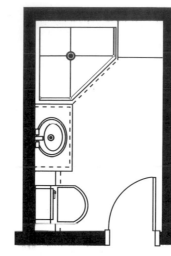

WITH MODERN ACCENTS

A bath that cleans up easily is a luxury in itself. Accessible storage space always helps, but smooth surfaces that wipe dry are a big plus. These are especially important features if the bath is shared with guests. The shimmering men's bath shown here looks good no matter who makes use of it.

The floating vanity has four deep drawers, ideal for large bottles and extra hand towels. An undermount sink prevents soap and other residue from accumulating along the top rim. The gray-and-white vanity is dressed up with a classy arched faucet and square-shaped door hardware.

EASY TO CLEAN

A speckled design helps conceal dirt (left), although the solid-surfacing counter-top cleans up easily when guests are expected. Four deep drawers are great for storing taller essentials and bulky objects. Designer: Carolyn B. Thomas/NKBA Design Competition 1992. Sink: Kohler.

NEOANGLE SHOWER

Having limited space to work with, the designer opted for a neoangle shower (right) and a vanity shelf to the side. The glass shower enclosure makes the contemporary bath seem more spacious. Countertop: DuPont Corian.

MAKEOVERS FOR TWO

Cosmetic changes can make a huge difference in the look and feel of a bathroom. In the crisp gray-and-white men's bath featured on this page, a whole new style was introduced as the result of a major overhaul. Although the bath seems bigger to its owner than the original, no space was added. White fixtures and faux-painted cabinets breathe new life into the space.

   The second bathroom challenged the designer to update it while staying faithful to the home's other rooms and architecture. What a difference a little paint makes! The vanity for one, painted to look like rich mahogany wood, matches the window. Other changes, like the addition of the light fixture, lend a classic touch. Patterned wallcovering and fabric add some brighter colors to this masculine space.

TILE WALL

White tile (above) in straight rows and diagonal patterns opens up the tub area.

EXTRA STORAGE

Two narrow wall cabinets (above) take the place of an old medicine cabinet. A center mirror is suitable for grooming. Fixtures: Kohler.

PAINTED ACCENTS

The cabinets (left) are hand painted in a soft gray finish and highlighted by faux marble trim in green. A hardwood floor is just what the homeowners wanted. Designer: Cynthia Kaspar.

FAUX MAHOGANY

A fresh coat of paint on the vanity and wood window (left) creates the look of mahogany. The diamond pattern of the wallcovering and skirting adds elegance to the room. Designer: Boxwood House. Wallpaper, fabric: Osborne & Little. Light fixture: Dason.

ALL THAT GLITTERS

A shower and toilet (below) are found on one side of the master-suite setup. "Her" bath, located on the other side of the vanity wall, includes a tub. Designer: Janine Jordan, CKD, IIDA.

These two baths are perfect examples of how smooth, shiny surfaces can light up a room, whether it's big or small.

A wall of mirrors creates the optical illusion of more space in the bath on this page. More than that, though, it's a real attention-getter that adds impact. This bath is part of a suite consisting of entirely separate sides for "him" and "her." They share a common wall, but that's all. "His" side has the shower, while "hers" has the tub.

Using all one color—other than white—on the main surfaces is so rarely done that it's refreshing. Just be sure to select a color that you won't tire of quickly. The green backdrop in the second bath lets the magnificent details of a white toilet and bidet stand out. While a designer might tell you not to be afraid to expand on color, the opposite is also true—don't be afraid of sticking to just one.

Faux marble (right) decorates this impressive space from head to toe. The square shelves are a modern contrast to the classically designed bidet and toilet. Tile: Laufen International.

SPACE-ENHANCING ANGLES

Walls are often overlooked when creating a new bathroom. Of course, one may be knocked down or added. Decorating with a fresh new color or pattern is commonplace, but a lot more can be done with walls.

Just look at this Art Deco bathroom. The angled walls add visual interest and spacious areas for the fixtures. A false wall of sorts was built behind the tub to create a flat plane for the two-person whirlpool. The half wall becomes a display area for pretty ceramics and makes towels accessible. Taking advantage of unused space, the designer recessed a television into one of the walls.

The bath's cool peach tones are crisply contrasted by rich burgundy fixtures. The white ceiling makes the room appear even more dramatic. The final touch is a modern light fixture descending from above.

ON DISPLAY

Tile molding (above), in a deeper shade than the soft peach used throughout the bath, creates a decorative edge on open shelves.
Designer: John A. Buscarello, ASID. Tile: Hastings Tile & Il Bagno Collection.

PRIVATE QUARTERS

Although all the burgundy fixtures are out in the open (left), they're nicely spaced. Angles help the design feel roomy and uncluttered.
Fixtures, fittings, accessories: Kohler.

TUB FOR TWO

Two bathers can enjoy the soothing waters of a whirlpool tub (left) in this curved corner model. Television sets are becoming more popular in master baths. Light fixture: American Glass Light. TV: RCA.

CLEAN AND UNCLUTTERED

If you're a person who thinks less is more, don't be talked into adding bright or frilly decorations to your new bath. Crisp lines and shapes can be interesting enough. Remember, the bath you pay for is the one you have to live with day in and day out. The end product should be exactly what you want, right down to the last detail.

Simplicity is the theme of this contemporary bath design. The white double-vanity top rests on chrome tubing for support. There's no built-in storage space. The homeowner selected a piece of furniture to handle the task instead. Floor tile runs up around the tub and into the oversize shower for continuity. The color scheme is appropriately neutral.

OUT OF VIEW

Recessed storage (left) fills the need created when typical vanity-base cabinets are eliminated. The toilet has its own private room.
Architect: Lloyd Jafvert.

VANITY FOR TWO

The look might be minimal, but the design is packed with modern amenities. Dual vanities (right) continue to be more and more popular with homeowners.

BURSTING WITH SUNSHINE

A child's bath is a great place to try something you've always wanted, but didn't think you could get away with, in your formal master bath. You might start by selecting a favorite color and using it liberally. Kids' rooms are ideal spots for having fun.

This bath is covered with cheery yellow. Its bright design is something that will help young ones get going in the morning. The white vanity is suited for the many things kids need in the bathroom. There's even a built-in hamper, which will encourage keeping dirty clothes off the floor.

TUB & SHOWER

An all-inclusive tub-shower combo (below) makes sense when space doesn't allow for separate fixtures. Shower wall: Swan. Toilet: American Standard.

COLOR COORDINATES

Yellow and white are used throughout the bath, right down to the fittings (above). The color scheme is great for kids of all ages. Designer: Marilyn Tourtellot, ASID. Stylist: Susan Andrews. Faucet: Delta.

DELUXE VANITY

This floor is too pretty to cover with dirty clothes. That's why a built-in hamper (left) comes in handy. With the sink at the far end, the countertop is free for someone else to use. Tile: Porcelanosa. Sink: Kohler.

PRETTY IN PINK

Soft pastels add a fairytale charm to the raised-panel cabinets (right). Florals are a delight in this girl's bath.
Designer: Arthur Barbanell, ASID.

DESIGNS KIDS WON'T OUTGROW

Safety is very important when designing any bathroom. In a bath used by kids, it should be the driving force of the design. Select a tub or shower with a slip-resistant bottom. Look for faucets with temperature-control valves to prevent accidental scaldings. Add a grab bar—today's versions come in many different colors and styles. Keep outlets far from water. Kids might not truly understand electrical hazards.

The two baths shown here, one for a girl and the other for a boy, each have touches of fantasy. A shade of pink decorates the one vanity with feminine delight. Glass block and bold accents add impact to the boy's bath. What's especially nice about these two spaces is that they're not overdone. Thus, the designs continue to meet the children's needs as they grow up.

FOR THE BOYS

A bird motif on the stucco walls (above) is a whimsical treat. Glass block lets natural light in, without sacrificing privacy. Vanity: Laufen International. Faucet: Delta. Recessed medicine cabinet: NuTone.

NEOANGLE SHOWER

An angled design (right) offers the extra room a growing boy needs when showering. There's a regular showerhead and a handheld spray inside. Designer: Jackie Naylor Interiors, Inc.

SHOWER COMFORT

This shower (above) may be striking, but there's even more here than meets the eye. A double door keeps water inside and makes entering and exiting the tub-shower combination free from restrictions. *Designer: Kitchens by Krengel.*

AT THE SINK

A temperature-control feature (left) is a must on faucets used by children and older people. Countertops and cabinets mix solid surfacing and laminate. *Laminate, solid surfacing: Ralph Wilson Plastics.*

TWO-VANITY BATH

Today's bathroom plans often include separate grooming areas that make simultaneous use of the bath more comfortable. It's an amenity most often found in master baths, but occasionally used in other bath spaces as well.

The designer of this colorful bath made sure that two kids could use the room at the same time. There's plenty of separate storage space. Two toilets and two sinks are on opposite sides of the room.

The colors used on each side of the room are the same, but the color blocks are rearranged. In the center of the bath, a sunny yellow tub platform fits right in. Glass doors open in the center, which makes getting in and out of the tub-shower combination safer.

· STORAGE SPACE

Its bold colors might grab the spotlight, but this vanity (right) is really functional. Wall cabinets hold items used less frequently.

OPEN SHELVING

The color scheme of the first vanity is reversed here (above). Open shelving will help keep towels and other necessities close at hand— and off the floor.

BRIGHT COLORS

The patterns may be different (right), but the colors remain the same: red, black, and white. *Stylist: Susan Andrews.*

BLACK, RED, AND BOLD ALL OVER

Kids' or family baths are great places to have some fun with color. Youngsters are usually receptive to unique designs and bright shades. There are many ways to introduce color into the bath. Wallcoverings, door hardware, and throw rugs are all easily updated or replaced when you want to make some cosmetic changes.

This black-and-white bath has red accents throughout. It's appealing to users of all ages. High-gloss cabinets have a contemporary look, especially with red drawer pulls and a white solid-surfacing countertop. No matter what counter material you use, customization allows you an opportunity to be creative.

Matching wallpaper features interesting vertical stripes mixed with random black-and-white bubbles. A checkerboard floor fits right in. Fancy tilework in the shower adds interest. With a glass enclosure, the shower is open for viewing in and out.

A playful geometric pattern (above) decorates the shower walls. The glass shower door keeps the design on display. Tile: Latco.

Angles on the countertop (right) add interest to the striking vanity. With an integral sink, the vanity is easily wiped clean. Designer: Sharlette John.

DESIGNS THAT ARE FUN—AND SAFE

Age plays a role in planning a bathroom for kids. It's not so much how old the children are now. The tricky part is figuring out what they will want a few years from now. A lot sooner than you'll want to remodel, the children's needs and tastes will be different.

Vanities and fixtures that are easy to work around are good to start with. Don't be afraid to go for invigorating accents. These two baths use an appealing backdrop for adults and children of all ages. Though there's nothing that screams "child's space," the look is fresh and fun—like kids. Both rooms are also up to date and safe.

Special features in both bathrooms will continue to meet the needs of a family for years to come. The one bath has a special raised sink for shampooing one's hair. Two lavatories in the other allow for side-by-side grooming.

DOUBLE VANITY

Kids can get ready for school together every morning at this large vanity (right). The designer specified laminate cabinets with "touch" closure to eliminate hardware. Designer: Gary E. White, CKD, CBD. Countertop: DuPont Corian.

TWO SINKS

Raising part of the counter and adding a second sink (right) is a great idea. With a detachable spray, the sink is ready to be used for shampooing. Designer: Janine Jordan, CKD, IIDA.

BIG IDEAS FOR SMALL ONES

Bathrooms can be pretty intimidating for kids. The designs aren't usually geared to children's special needs. Turning on the water and washing hands are often accomplished only with some fancy tip-toe action. Whether you're designing a bath especially for children or one for family members or guests that will be used by kids, too, be sure to think ahead.

Both bathrooms shown here feature friendly products and ideas that encourage kids to be independent. Single-lever faucets and drawer pulls are easy for small hands to operate. Just make sure the faucet has an antiscald device built in. Pullout steps, like those in the bath on this page, bring kids up to counter height.

Each room has ample lighting. This is especially important when tending to little cuts and bruises. Kids like to watch themselves. Plenty of mirrors encourage good grooming habits.

IDEAL HEIGHT

Two pullout steps (right) bring kids to the proper height. The built-in tissue box is suitable for the whole family. Designers: Avra Bershad Pressman, ASID, and Nadine Nemec. Cabinets: Wood-Mode. Fixtures, fittings: Kohler. Tile: American Olean. Mirrored cabinet: Robern.

GROOMING SPACE

Plenty of light and mirroring (left) keep this design bright and inviting. Designer: Nancy Ruzicka. Stylist: Susan Andrews. Sink: Kohler. Faucet: Delta. Shower wall: Swan. Tile: Porcelanosa.

IT'S TIME
TO FRESHEN UP

Powder rooms come in all shapes and sizes. Most often they're located near the main living space for the convenience of guests and family members alike. Powder rooms may reflect the interior of the rest of the home, but there's no reason why you can't try something a little bit different.

Every powder room needs sufficient lighting for a quick touch-up. Little extras, like color-coordinated hand towels and ornate accessories, are suitable finishing touches.

ON THE WALLS

Guests who come to wash up are treated to springtime florals (above) in this traditional decor. Designer: Janet Alholm. Stylist: Susan Andrews. Sink: Kohler.

MODERN HINTS

Black and white invigorate a small space (right). Powder rooms are ideal spots for trying something a little bold. Designer: Geraldine Kaupp. Wallcovering, fabric: Clarence House. Fixtures: Kohler.

LIGHT & AIRY

Sunlight and creamy tile (above, left) provide a pretty backdrop for painted ivy patterns. Architect: Gayle Monahan, ASID.

EASY TO UPDATE

Coordinated wallcovering and fabric, like those used here (above, right), are warm and inviting. They're also easy to change when you want to create a new look. Designer: BJ Eichorn, ASID, IIDA. Wallcovering, fabric: Ralph Lauren.

WITH ANTIQUES

Elegant leaves showcase treasured pictures (left). The ornate mirror and sconce are antiques. Designer: Joan Gray. Wallcovering: Brunschwig & Fils. Fabric: Cowtan & Tout.

PERSONALITY ON DISPLAY

Anything goes in a powder room. The only real necessity is creating a space that's comfortable to use. Perhaps you can update your bath without doing a total remodeling project. Add a new pedestal sink. Fix those loose floor tiles. Replace the wallcovering.

The cream bath on the facing page was freshened up with new fixtures. The original floor stayed in place.

As the bath on this page shows, a powder room can be a nice place to showcase a hobby or interest. Elaborate wallcovering turns the space into a library of sorts.

WALLS OF BOOKS

This powder room (left) becomes a small reading room with its library-style wallcovering. The rich wood vanity resembles a fine, marble-topped desk.
Designer: Arthur Barbanell, ASID. Fittings: Sherle Wagner. Wallcovering: Brunschwig & Fils.

Simple decoration brightens this little bath (left). A new wallcovering updates the space, while maintaining its old-fashioned charm. The radiator cover is made of wood and covered with a painted and decorated metal grille. *Designer: Karen Houghton. Sconce, sink, fittings: Waterworks. Wallcovering: F. Schumacher & Company.*

BEYOND THE ORDINARY

In a powder room, the vanity becomes the focal point. Rather than go for a typical base cabinet/countertop/sink setup, have some fun. Here's the one spot in your home where friends and family members freshen up. A deluxe vanity will make them feel pampered.

The three one-of-a-kind vanities showcased here are dramatic. One goes for a futuristic look, while another resembles a Stone Age relic. Accent lighting creates steps on the third, a gray marblesque beauty. Other niceties in a powder room might include a telephone, open display shelves, and specialty mirrors for makeup application.

EXTRA STORAGE

A triple-mirrored wall unit and contemporary cabinets (right) offer plenty of space for bathroom essentials. A phone and a magazine rack are added comforts for guests. Designer: Doris Bahmann Amsterdam. Mirrored cabinet: Robern.

NATURAL LOOKS

This vanity (above) is an interesting mix of old and new. The stainless faucet and sink are high tech, while the countertop has stood the test of time. Designer: Jackie Naylor Interiors, Inc.

TRIPLE TIERS

Accent lighting (right) adds impact to the steps below this floating vanity. The black sink with gold detailing is a classy contrast. Designer: Janine Jordan, CKD, IIDA.

DISPLAY SHELF

A custom shelf (left) makes use of empty space while providing a pretty resting spot for vases.

NOT JUST FOR COMPANY

When you begin planning a new powder room, consider who will be using it before you make any decisions. If the bath is located close to the kitchen, living room, or family room, it's probably used more frequently than the home's full baths. And it's probably used by people who live in the house on a regular basis.

Every bath should suit the needs of those who use it most. The three shown here offer Victorian charm that blends with the decor beyond their four walls. Architectural details and lavish products make the spaces rich with elegance.

GARDEN BOUQUET

Wood molding and smoky blue, pink, and green accents (above) complement the adjoining study. Pleasant florals are always refreshing. Designer: Alvin Schneider Design.

CLASSIC RETREAT

If you've got the space and the budget, create a powder room that's a total retreat (right). Pink and white are cool and crisp in any decor. Designer: Jeanie Ziering. Fixtures, fittings, tile: Hastings Tile & Il Bagno Collection.

PEDESTAL LAV

When space is at a premium, a pedestal sink with a roomy surround (left) can work wonders. The pillared base and rope edging fit the bath's classic look. *Designer: Andrea Saches, Ltd. Sink, fittings: Sherle Wagner. Wallcovering: Uika Vaev-USA.*

RESOURCE DIRECTORY

ARCHITECTS/DESIGNERS:

Absolute Bath Boutique
Bridgewater Commons
400 Commmons Way
Bridgewater, NJ 08807

Accent on Design
2075 De La Cruz Blvd., #101
Santa Clara, CA 95050

Janet Alholm
3008 W. 117th St.
Leawood, KS 66209

Doris Bahmann Amsterdam
200 Winston Drive, #3103
Cliffside Park, NJ 07010

Susan Andrews
9642 Horton
Overland Park, KS 66207

Austin Patterson Associates
376 Pequot Ave.
P.O. Box 61
Southport, CT 06490

Jackie Balint, CKD
The Kitchen Collection
241 Avenida Del Norte
Redondo Beach, CA 90277

Arthur Barbanell, ASID
333 E. 84th St.
New York, NY 10028

Barbara E. Barton, CBD
Kitchensmith, Inc.
1198 N. Highland Ave.
Atlanta, GA 30306

Boxwood House
44 North Dean St.
Englewood, NJ 07631

Julie Boynton
JCB Interiors
1689 The Great Road
Skillman, NJ 08558

Randy Brandes
A & B Kitchens & Baths
279 Franklin Ave.
Wyckoff, NJ 07481

Marsha Broderick
Pink Ladies
5038 N. Parkway Calabasas, #400
Calabasas, CA 91302

John A. Buscarello, ASID
1 University Place
New York, NY 10003

Laura Chandler, IFDA
Laura Chandler Decorative
  Painting
4233 W. Howard Ave.
Kensington, MD 20895

Coastal Development &
  Investment, Inc.
P.O. Box 38290
Orlando, FL 32819

MollyAnne Conroy
Concepts II Ltd.
215 E. Baker St.
Costa Mesa, CA 92626

Craig Patterson & Associates
2345 Grand
Kansas City, MO 64108

Bahamon Dingman
1950 Massachusetts Ave.
Cambridge, MA 02140

Kathleen Donohue, CKD, CBD
Neil Kelly Designers/Remodelers
8101 S.W. Nimbus, Bldg. 11
Beaverton, OR 97219

Thomas F. Doty
International Kitchen & Bath
  Exchange
6588 Rogue View Court
Belmont, MI 49306

Connie Edwards, CKD
American Woodmark
P.O. Box 1980
Winchester, VA 22604

BJ Eichorn, ASID, IIDA
4454 Stateline
Kansas City, KS 66103

Ferne Goldberg Interior Design
611 Broadway, #516
New York, NY 10012

Carol Fox, ASID
Carol Fox Designs
1293 Calle de Madrid
Pacific Palisades, CA 90272

Merrie Fredericks, CKD, CBD
Design Concepts Plus, Inc.
49 W. Eagle Road
Havertown, PA 19083

Stephanie Gisoldi
Unique Kitchens & Baths
1715 S. Easton Road
Doylestown, PA 18901

Betsy Godfrey
329 Park Ave. S.
Winter Park, FL 32789

Katie Goldfarb, IFDA
Goldesigns by Katie Goldfarb
8520 Atwell Road
Potomac, MD 20854

Joan Gray
Grayson, Ltd.
266 Post Road E.
Westport, CT 06880

Timothy Huber
Designer Cabinetry
4350 E. Camelback Road, #110C
Phoenix, AZ 85108

Jackie Naylor Interiors, Inc.
4287 Glengary Drive
Atlanta, GA 30342

Joan Halperin Interior Design
401 E. 80th St.
New York, NY 10021

Sharlette John
1153 E.E. Riwe Road
Lee's Summit, MO 64086

Jonna Avella Graphic Design
900 East Indiantown Road, #207
Jupiter, FL 33477

Linder Jones
Linder Design/Builders
939 San Rafael Ave.
Mountain View, CA 94043

Janine Jordan, CKD, IIDA
JJ Interiors
Kitchen & Bath Design by Janine
P.O. Box 5130
Chapel Hill, NC 27514

Tammy & Roslyn Kaplan
Images in Design
23 Mendell Ave.
Cranford, NJ 07016

Karen Houghton Interiors
41 N. Broadway
Nyack, NY 10960

Cynthia Kaspar
Interior Accents
43 Fairview Farm Road
West Redding, CT 06896

Geraldine Kaupp
25 West Road
Short Hills, NJ 07078

Leo Kelsey, CKD, CBD
600 General Bruce Drive
Temple, TX 76501

Sachi Kemeta
600 General Bruce Drive
Temple, TX 76501

Thomas D. Kling, CKD
Thomas D. Kling, Inc.
2474 N. George St.
York, PA 17402

Holly K'Lynn
A.D.A.P.T. International Design
28 Strawberry Ridge
Ridgefield, CT 06877

Thomas F. Leckstrom, CKD
Designs Unlimited, Inc.
5 Parker Road
Osterville, MA 02655

Victoria Leist
Kitchen & Bath Design
1505 E. Francisco Blvd.
San Rafael, CA 94901

Lindal Cedar Homes
10201 Lee Highway, #225
Fairfax, VA 22030

George Magyar, CBD
19 Malvern Road
Norwood, MA 02862

Marlise Karlin Designs
10100 Santa Monica Blvd., #1300
Los Angeles, CA 90067

Gayle Monahan, ASID
24 Butterfield Road
Newtown, CT 06470

Nadine Nemec, ABID
Walnut Hill, Unit 26
731 Wynnewood Road
Ardmore, PA 19003

Kenneth Neumann, FAIA
Neumann Smith and Associates
400 Galleria Officentre, #555
Southfield, MI 48034

Stephanie Harrington O'Neill
90 Park St. W.
Windsor, Ontario N9A7A8
Canada

Sharon Overstake, CKD
WmOhs Showrooms
2900 E. Sixth Ave.
Denver, CO 80206

Shelley Patterson
Linder Design/Builders
939 San Rafael Ave.
Mountain View, CA 94043

Avra Bershad Pressman, ABID
Walnut Hill, Unit 26
731 Wynnewood Road
Ardmore, PA 19003

Jeffrey Scott Queripel
Queripel Interiors
93 W. Bridge St.
New Hope, PA 18938

Jane Redfield Schwartz
Kelter Schwartz Design
801 S. Adams Road
Birmingham, MI 48301

Pat Robinson, ASID
2 Broken Bow Lane
Rolling Hills Estates, CA 90274

Nancy Ruzicka
5828 Pembroke Circle
Mission Hills, KS 66208

Martha Sasso
S.J. Pappas
718 Old Colony Road
Meriden, CT 06450

Schaerer Design, Inc.
280 Daines St., #200
Birmingham, MI 48009

Marilee Schempp, ASID
Design I
The Summit Opera House
497 Springfield Ave.
Summit, NJ 07907

Deborah Schroll
Gordon Schroll
ABC Kitchens & Baths
454 Northwest Highway
Des Plaines, IL 60016

Ann M. Schwalm
Lamperti Associates
1241 Andersen Drive
San Rafael, CA 94901

Rona Spiegal, ASID
RJS Interiors
2 Summit St.
Englewood Cliffs, NJ 07632

Terra Designs
241 E. Blackwell St.
Dover, NJ 07801

Kenneth J. Thelen, CKD, AIA
Thelen Kitchen & Bath Studios
5566 Chamblee Dunwoody Road
Atlanta, GA 30338

Carolyn B. Thomas
Melvin C. Keller, Inc.
11500 Schuylkill Road
Rockville, MD 20852

Nancy Thornett
Nancy Thornett Associates, Inc.
6701 Democracy Blvd.
Bethesda, MD 20817

Thomas Trzcinski, CKD, CBD
Kitchen & Bath Concepts of
    Pittsburgh
7901 Perry Highway
Pittsburgh, PA 15237

TSI Development
900 E. Indiantown Road, #207
Jupiter, FL 33477

Debra K. Ureel
CBI Design Professionals
4050 W. Maple Road, #215
Bloomfield Hills, MI 48301

Van-Martin Rowe
195 S. Parkwood Ave.
Pasadena, CA 91107

Wayne Walega, CKD
Walega Associates
92 North St.
Mattapoisett, MA 02739

Gary E. White
Kitchen & Bath Design
1000 Bristol St. N.
Newport Beach, CA 92660

Robert I. Wine, AIA
4050 W. Maple, #106
Bloomfield Hills, MI 48301

SOURCES:

Allmilmo Corporation
70 Clinton Road
P.O. Box 629
Fairfield, NJ 07006

Amaru Tile
73 Sherwood Ave.
Farmingdale, NY 11735

American Glass Light
979 Third Ave.
New York, NY 10022

American Olean
1000 Cannon Ave.
Lansdale, PA 19446-0271

American Standard
1 Centennial Plaza
Piscataway, NJ 08855-6820

American Woodmark
P.O. Box 1980
Winchester, VA 22604

Armstrong
P.O. Box 3001
Lancaster, PA 17604

Baldinger Architectural
    Lighting, Inc.
19-02 Steinway St.
Astoria, NY 11105

Baldwin Harware Corp.
841 E. Wyomissing Blvd.
Box 15048
Redding, PA 19612

Basco
Q595 Palmer Ave.
University Park, IL 60466

Benjamin Moore
51 Chestnut Ridge Road
Montvale, NJ 07645

Bertch Cabinetry
1205 Peters Drive
Waterloo, IA 50703

Bob Mitchell Designs
Borden, Inc.
Box 567
San Gabriel, CA 91778

The Broadway Collection
1010 W. Santa Fe
P.O. Box 1210
Olathe, KS 66051-1210

Brunschwig & Fils
979 Third Ave.
New York, NY 10022

Clairson International/Closet Maid
720 S.W. 17th St.
Ocala, FL 32674

Color Tree Designs
Division of Eisenhart Wallcoverings
P.O. Box 464
400 Pine St.
Hanover, PA 17331

Cooper Lighting
Halo Division
400 Busse Road
Elk Grove Village, IL 60007

Country Floors
15 E. 16th St.
New York, NY 10003

Dal-Tile Corporation
P.O. Box 17130
Dallas, TX 75217

Delta
P.O. Box 40980
Indianapolis, IN 46280

Dornbracht
6687 Jimmy Carter Blvd.
Norcross, GA 30871

DuPont Corian
1007 Market St.
Wilmington, DE 19898

Dura Supreme
300 Dura Drive
Howard Lake, MN 55349

Eljer
3 Gateway Center
Pittsburgh, PA 15222

Esquema Collection
8275 N.W. 36th St.
Miami, FL 33166

Fieldcrest
1271 Avenue of the Americas
New York, NY 10020

Fieldstone
P.O. Box 109
Northwood, IA 50459

Floor Gres Ceramiche
Via Canaletto 24
41042 Fiorano, MO
Italy

Florida Tile
P.O. Box 447
Lakeland, FL 33802

F. Schumacher & Co.
79 Madison Ave.
New York, NY 10016

Fuda Marble
261 Route 46 W.
Elmwood Park, NJ 07652

Glass Products International
Box 313
Carbondale, PA 18407

G.M. Ketcham Co., Inc.
7331 William Ave., #600
Allentown, PA 18106

Grohe
241 Covington Drive
Bloomington, IL 60108

Hansgrohe
2840 Research Park Drive, #100
Soquel, CA 95073

Harden Furniture
Mill Pond Way
McConnellsville, NY 13401

Hastings Tile & Il Bagno Collection
30 Commercial St.
Freeport, NY 11520

Hydro Systems
P.O. Box 135
Sunrise Beach, MO 65079

International Tile Design Studio
9324 Corbin Ave.
Northridge, CA 91324

Jacuzzi
2121 N. California Blvd., #475
Walnut Creek, CA 94596

Jado Group
P.O. Box 1329
Camarillo, CA 93011

Kallista
2701 Merced St.
San Leandro, CA 94577

Kohler
Kohler, WI 53044

Latco Products
2943 Gleneden St.
Los Angeles, CA 90039

Laufen International
4942 E. 66th St. N.
Tulsa, OK 74117-1802

Madison Design Group
1700 Stutz Drive
Troy, MI 48084

Michigan Tile & Marble Co.
9317 Freeland
Detroit, MI 48228

Moen Inc.
377 Woodland Ave.
Elyria, OH 44036-2111

Myson
P.O. Box 5446
Embrey Industrial Park
Falmouth, VA 22403

Nemo Tile
48 East 21st St.
New York, NY 10003

NuTone
P.O. Box 1580
Cincinnati, OH 45201

Osborne & Little
979 Third Ave.
New York, NY 10022

Pewabic Society
10125 E. Jefferson
Detroit, MI 48228

Phylrich
100 N. Orange Drive
Los Angeles, CA 90038

Pionite Laminate
1 Pionite Road
Auburn, ME 04210

Pittsburgh Corning
800 Presque Isle Drive
Pittsburgh, PA 15239-2724

Ralph Lauren
1185 Avenue of the Americas
New York, NY 10036

RCA
Thompson Consumer Electronics
600 N. Sherman Drive
Indianapolis, IN 46201-2598

Robern
1648 Winchester Road
Bensalem, PA 19020

Rutt Custom Cabinetry
1564 Main St.
P.O. Box 129
Goodville, PA 17528

Sherle Wagner
60 E. 89th St.
New York, NY 10022

ShowerLux
1380 Birchmont Road
Scarborough, Ontario
M1P 2E6 Canada

SieMatic
886 Town Center Drive
Langhorne, PA 19047

Smallbone
886 Town Center Drive
Langhorne, PA 19047

Southwestern Ceramic Tile
 & Marble Co.
5525 Gaines St.
San Diego, CA 92110

Steamist
1 Altman Drive
Rutherford, NJ 07070

Stroheim & Romann
155 E. 56th St.
New York, NY 10022

Summitville
P.O. Box 73
Summitville, OH 43962

Swan Corporation
1 City Center, #2300
St. Louis, MO 63101

Timberlake Cabinet Co.
P.O. Box 1990
Winchester, VA 22604

Uika Vacv-USA
305 E. 63rd St.
New York, NY 10021

Velux-America, Inc.
P.O. Box 3208
Greenwood, SC 29648

Villeroy & Bach
41 Madison Ave.
New York, NY 10016

Virginia Tile Co.
24404 Indoplex Circle
Farmington Hills, MI 48335

Walker Zanger
8901 Bradley Ave.
Sun Valley, CA 91352

Watercolors, Inc.
Garrison, NY 10524

Waverly
Division of F. Schumacher & Co.
79 Madison Ave.
New York, NY 10016

Wenzel
P.O. Box 7048A
St. Louis, MO 63177

Wilsonart
600 General Bruce Drive
Temple, TX 76501

Wood-Mode
1 Second St.
Cramer, PA 17833